Analyzing
Social Problems

Viewpoints in Sociology

Analyzing
Social Problems

Jerome G. Manis
Western Michigan University

Praeger Publishers
New York

Published in the United States of America in 1976
by Praeger Publishers, Inc.
111 Fourth Avenue, New York, N.Y. 10003

Library of Congress Cataloging in Publication Data

Manis, Jerome G
     Analyzing social problems.

     (Viewpoints in sociology)
     Bibliography: p. 172
     Includes index.
     1. Sociology—Methodology. 2. Social problems.
I. Title
HM24.M25   301'.07'2   75–36203
ISBN 0–275–22740–5
ISBN 0–275–85530–9 pbk.

Printed in the United States of America

Foreword

ARTHUR J. VIDICH

The Viewpoints in Sociology Series is designed to present to the beginning student a sense of the sociological attitude and an appreciation of the significant problems of our world. In this volume, Professor Manis addresses himself to the question, *What is a social problem?* Beginning students are likely to think that there is a simple answer to this basic question, but they, as well as advanced students, will learn from Professor Manis that his question is deceptively simple. Contrary to what we might suspect, specialists who have devoted their attention to this subject do not have an easy answer to the question. As is the case in all fields of scientific inquiry, investigators find that basic questions are the most difficult to answer.

Books about social problems in American society have been frequently influenced in their orientation by the Protestant and social reformist origins of American sociology, and the ministerial training of many early sociologists. As a result, the ethical and moral standards of Protestantism have provided the implicit standards for defining social problems in American sociology. Under these standards, social approval was given to the virtues of honesty, charity, sobriety, fidelity, monogamy, heterosexuality, hard and useful work, self-control, self-discipline, and cooperation with community standards of respectability. Therefore, by a simple process of reversal, dishonesty and violence, divorce, infidelity, homosexuality, prostitution, illegitimacy, suicide, laziness, unemployment, loss of self-control through alcohol or drugs, the breakdown of self-discipline brought about by the cultivation of the "inner self," and in general the refusal to accept existing social attitudes became social problems.

The earlier sociologists who established the pattern for the study of social problems were primarily midwestern and middle class in their origins and came from small or middle-sized towns. Thus, their attitudes were shaped by a society both preurban and preindustrial in comparison with contemporary society, which is essentially urban, industrial, and corporate. This transformation in the structure of our society and in the quality of our lives has been paralleled by changes in the moral and ethical codes by which we define social problems.

We now live in a world of rapidly changing life styles, sexual styles, and cultural expression. Society faces such problems as environmental pollution, widespread white-collar crime, uncontrolled growth of industrial corporations, and threats of nuclear destruction, and these newer problems have not yet been clearly and unambiguously defined as social problems. It is because we lack standards of choice acceptable to everyone that ours is a world of multiple moralities and ethics. Under these conditions, how do we define a social problem?

Many sociologists have attempted to answer this question and have often disagreed about the answer. While science may be able to specify the rational course of action necessary to the solution of a problem, as for example the making of nuclear weapons, science has no way of telling us whether or not we should make them in the first place. The social values of the scientist, or any other expert for that matter, cannot be proved to be better than those of the layman. Yet, Professor Manis is not satisfied to accept the idea that social problems cannot be studied scientifically. With the attitude of the scientist, he assesses his problem and attempts to find a solution. He reviews the major approaches to the study of social problems under the categories *social pathology, social disorganization, value conflicts, deviance,* and *public opinion.* All these approaches are currently in use, and Professor Manis is careful to present each viewpoint with care and thoroughness before presenting his own case. As a result, we are given a thorough grounding in the field, and *Analyzing Social Problems* serves not only as an introduction to the field but also as a systematic review of it. Professor Manis presents his own novel solution in a way that is not only impressive but path-breaking for students of social problems.

Preface

"Theirs not to reason why,/Theirs but to do and die"—
stirring words from "The Charge of the Light Brigade."
In this famed poem, Alfred Lord Tennyson gave voice to
popular sentiments of his time. Britons were thrilled by
the image of their brave cavalrymen attacking an en-
trenched enemy. Valor in combat was an esteemed virtue
and obeying orders without question an accepted duty.

A different view of the battle is presented in *The Reason
Why* (Woodham-Smith, 1947). The author asserts that the
attack was the direct result of misunderstood orders. She
traces the roots of the confusion to the British system of
military leadership of that era, in which aristocrats were
permitted to purchase their way into high military positions. Having used this avenue to leadership of the Light
Brigade, the commanding generals were untrained, inex-
perienced, and irresponsible rivals for fame and superiority. The outcome was a useless waste of many lives.

Can we learn from that foolish tragedy? Are there lessons to be learned from the Vietnam War, the Watergate
cover-up, secret assassination plots, an energy crisis, poverty, crime, and environmental pollution? Asking these

questions does not guarantee answers. Without good questions, however, we cannot expect good answers. Such answers may help us to avoid or to solve our serious social problems.

My reason for writing this book is a concern about our customary ways of looking at social problems. We live in a world with a variety of troubles and issues, and popular and governmental responses to these conditions range from apathy to zealotry. The responses are often based upon inadequate knowledge and conflicting values.

During the 1960s we waged a brief, hastily conceived, and unsuccessful War on Poverty. More common is the neglect of malnutrition, inadequate health care, and other deprivations of the poor.

Some states have imposed up to twenty-year mandatory prison terms on youths convicted of possession of small amounts of marihuana. Yet, corrupt politicians and businessmen have been penalized with small fines and suspended sentences.

Our many failures to deal with social problems imply the need for new approaches and techniques. This book is an attempt to meet that need. In it, I propose changes in our ways of identifying, assessing, and resolving social problems. The knowledge-values of science, explained later, are my guide in this enterprise. Like all scientific interpretations, these views are open to discussion, criticism, and correction. Readers will decide their merit.

In Chapter 1, I review traditional answers to the question "What is a social problem?" Many of the answers distill down to one, namely, whatever many group members consider undesirable. If we accept this perspective, however, we may overlook some critical conditions or may concentrate our attention upon unimportant or imaginary ones. I propose an alternative definition based upon scientific knowledge-values.

Chapter 2 deals with the ongoing controversy in science and philosophy over the relationship between facts and values. Many sociologists assert that, as scientists, they must be neutral and value-free. I contend that there are flaws in this claim, a view I share with others. I suggest that the knowledge-values of science can guide sociology in deciding what is harmful and what is not. I do *not* suggest that these views be imposed on society.

In Chapter 3, I discuss procedures that can help us identify social problems. The chapter includes a discussion of the relevance of some important sociological theories for the study of social problems. Also considered are the views of group members, of experts, and of science itself. My aim is to distinguish spurious from "real" social problems.

The basic purpose of Chapter 4 is to distinguish minor from serious social problems. Some say that the extent of public concern is the appropriate measure of seriousness. My criteria are the actual consequences of social conditions. With this standard in mind, I describe and examine sociological methods of obtaining and interpreting data about social problems.

In the final chapter, which is concerned with prevention and solutions, I point out the limitations as well as the potential benefits of applying the knowledge-values of science. Coping with social problems requires awareness, not merely by the scientific community, but also by society itself. Only an active society, one committed to improved understanding and action, can be expected to overcome its problems.

I owe much to the writers whose publications I have cited in the book. Complete source information is listed alphabetically in the reference section at the back of the book, and each chapter concludes with a brief number of pertinent readings.

Herbert Blumer and Robert K. Merton are distinguished teachers who have greatly influenced my thinking about sociology. They are leading exponents of different theories (see Chapter 3) that have stimulated my current ideas about social problems.

Deeply appreciated are the suggestions and criticisms of colleague-friends. Charles B. Keely, Bernard N. Meltzer, and Stanley S. Robin read and helped very much. Among the other particularly helpful readers have been James J. Bosco, Chester L. Hunt, Subhash Sonnad, Morton O. Wagenfeld, and Lewis Walker.

A number of students have discussed and debated some portions of the present volume. Two former students, R. Greg Emerton and Paul A. Dorsey, read and criticized earlier versions of my views. Robert E. Manis located source materials and offered many suggestions.

To series editor Arthur J. Vidich go my thanks for the gratifying appraisal of the manuscript and for specific recommendations. The prompt, efficient preparation of the book by the staff of Praeger Publishers, particularly by editor James F. Bergin, is much appreciated.

Lisa A. Manis helped me to clear my mind of outdated notions and to concentrate upon important issues. My wife, Laura Glance Manis, is the next-to-the-last mentioned and a most important influence upon this book. She read, listened, advised, and encouraged. Above all, her actions demonstrate to me that advanced knowledge and human values can combine to solve problems.

What have I done? I have studied, thought, argued, written, and rewritten. The clash of ideas in my mind is the direct source of the book. Appraising the contents is the task of the reader.

J.G.M.

Contents

1
What Is a Social Problem?

"Do you think the schools should require boys to keep their hair cut short?" Your answer, perhaps, is like mine —NO! The response of many Americans to this specific question during the 1960s was quite different. When a national survey was conducted in the fall of 1965, 80 percent of the sample population agreed that the schools should require short hair (Gallup, 1972; 1965). Expulsion from athletic teams, classes, and high schools was a widespread penalty for those young men who refused to cut their hair.

We need to know why so many people were disturbed by a change in hairstyles. Sociologists specializing in the study of social change, social psychology, public opinion, and deviant behavior have sought explanations for such attitudes and actions. I shall consider some of these interpretations in later sections.

Our concern is with a related question: Was long hair a social problem in 1965? To answer this question, we need to define the term *social problem*. According to a recent dictionary of sociological concepts, a social problem is "any undesirable condition or situation that is judged by an influential number of persons within a community to be intolerable and to require group action toward constructive reform" (Theodorson and Theodorson, 1969:392). Most textbooks on social problems contain similar definitions. Unfortunately, the accepted definition leads to certain dubious conclusions.

A central feature of current sociological definitions of social problems is that "influential" (or significant or large) numbers of people consider some condition, situation, or behavior as undesirable. When 80 percent of the members of a society believe that long hair is not to be tolerated, we must conclude that long hair appears to be a social problem—at least, according to the definition. Despite their definitions, however, social-problem texts have *not* been concerned with long hair. You may ask, Why not? I have no certain explanation, but I believe that sociologists ignore the definition when the "social problem" seems ridiculous or unimportant to them.

If a social problem exists whenever many people believe it exists, then should we say that its significance depends on the specific number of concerned people? Indeed, this reasonable inference from the definition is suggested by the authors of an article in the *Handbook on the Study of Social Problems* (Tallman and McGee, 1971:42): "The magnitude of a social problem is greatest when large numbers of people are deeply stirred and thereby moved to action." Presumably, long hair would be a major or important social problem, since so many people were in opposition to the new hairstyle. Your reaction, like mine, is probably like that of Alice in Wonderland, "ridiculoser and ridiculoser." Not very grammatical, but an appropriate judgment.

Paradigms and Anomalies

Before considering other possible definitions, let us further examine the current definition. Our procedure will follow certain ideas suggested by Thomas S. Kuhn, a historian of science. For Kuhn (1970), every scientific specialization is guided by interpretations based on available knowledge and research findings. These shared interpretations help to make sense out of complex topics while encouraging research questions within the accepted framework of analysis.

Kuhn uses the term *scientific paradigm* to refer to the accepted way of conceiving the subject matter of a scientific specialty. The "wave" conception of physical optics is one illustration of a scientific paradigm. The "public opinion" definition of social problems is, I believe, another example.

The basic features of a "Kuhn paradigm" have been described: "(1) It represents a radically new conceptualization of phenomena; (2) It suggests a new research strategy or methodological procedure for gathering empirical evidence to support the paradigm; (3) It tends to suggest new problems for solution; (4) Application of the new paradigm frequently explains phenomena that previous paradigms were unable to explain" (Reynolds, 1971:22). Not-so-new conceptualizations have been called *paradigm variations* (Reynolds, 1971:32).

The paradigms adopted by scientists during their day tend to be viewed as *normal science*. Thus, Newton's formulation of the laws of motion were considered by most scientists for several centuries as an appropriate way of explaining matter and energy. The implications of a widely accepted paradigm tend to generate new propositions, researches, and findings. Some of these outcomes may not "fit" satisfactorily into the paradigm. Others may even appear as contradictions. *Scientific anomalies* are the unexpected, contradictory, or doubtful products of new research or theorizing. The outcome may be the development of a new paradigm.

The current definition of social problems—conditions considered undesirable by many people—is a sociological paradigm that has led to apparent anomalies. On the basis of the definition, we must consider long hair as a social problem. Certainly, long hair bothered many people and we need to understand the basis for their discontent. Perhaps they believed that boys who refused to shorten their hair were revolutionists, drug abusers, or "hippies." The question is, whether sociologists should accept these beliefs as grounds for identifying long hair as a social problem.

Those who doubt the conclusion that long hair was "really" a social problem will consider it to be an anomaly of the paradigm. Those who question whether large numbers of concerned people make a condition into a social problem of great magnitude will perceive another anomaly. In other words, the definition of social problems requires the acceptance of public beliefs concerning trivial or imaginary troubles. The public opinion paradigm of social problems cannot resolve these (and other) anomalies.

Up, Down, and Up Again

To help understand present-day concerns with social problems, we shall briefly review their changes in American sociology. Although the origins of sociology can be traced to Europeans—particularly August Comte, Herbert Spencer, Emile Durkheim, Georg Simmel, and Max Weber—our focus will be upon the United States. Not only has sociology been developed furthest here, but also much emphasis has been placed on the problems of society. Indeed, sociology has been described as the "American science."

Many of the early American sociologists were drawn to the field because of their concern with poverty, crime, and urban slums. These founders of the field, frequently, were reformers, drawn from the ministry, charitable organizations, and journalism, as well as other social sciences. Courses dealing with sociology were introduced in the nineteenth century by departments of theology, philosophy, social science, and economics. The earliest courses were entitled "moral philosophy," "social ethics," "social science," "sociology," and "social problems." Their subject matter was concerned, largely, with the poor, drunkenness, orphans, and a variety of other "bad" conditions. Their goal, usually, was "social betterment."

However defined or named, social problems have been a central concern of sociology throughout most of its short existence. For a period of several decades, this concern was less pronounced. From about the mid-thirties to the mid-fifties, some sociologists argued that the concern with "undesirable conditions" was moralistic, unscientific, and premature (Merton, 1949:8). They argued that since science must be neutral and value-free, sociologists should avoid making the evaluations implicit in terms like social problems.

Since the 1960s there has been a strong resurgence of interest in social problems. In part this has occurred through the efforts of sociologists who founded the Society for the Study of Social Problems and the professional journal *Social Problems* (1953). Perhaps even more important were the influences of the War on Poverty, Vietnam, and racial conflicts. Sociologists raised questions about the presumed neutrality of science and the neglect of social problems.

The renewed concern has been accompanied by a reexamination of the underlying assumptions and the value premises of sociology. This concern is especially evident in the study of social problems. Textbooks and articles in professional journals are reviewing related concepts and raising questions about the prevailing definitions. We too are doing so.

In the following sections, I shall review the most widely used concepts pertaining to social problems. Specifically, I shall consider the following: social pathology, social disorganization, value-conflict, deviance, and public opinion. They are listed chronologically, that is, in the approximate time sequence in which they were initiated. All of them are still being applied by sociologists, though in varying extent and with varying definitions. At times they have been used in definitions of social problems, as types of social problems, and as preferred alternatives to the concept of social problems (see Rubington and Weinberg, 1971; Lowry, 1974).

Each of the five concepts will be viewed as a scientific paradigm—a way of conceiving phenomena with implications for action, theory, and research. I shall look at their basic assumptions, definitions, and possible shortcomings. My aim is to arrive at an improved perspective on social problems.

The Pathology Paradigm

In the nineteenth century, Darwin's theory had placed the human species in an evolutionary classification. The idea of evolution was not entirely new. What was new and significant was the concept of natural selection. According to Darwin, natural selection—survival of the fittest—was the basis for the gradual, continuing process that produced more adaptable and more complex organisms. The new paradigm of evolution not only had a major impact on biology but also influenced sociology.

For those sociologists who viewed the moralistic judgments of their nineteenth-century predecessors as biased and unscientific, the great progress in biology suggested more "objective" interpretations of social problems. To some, the problems appeared explainable as the product of "inferior stock," that is, defective, inadequate people. Crime, poverty, and ignorance were attributed to the lower classes, the recent immigrants from eastern and southern Europe, and the non-whites. To these sociologists, social pathology referred to defective, unhealthy human organisms. One of the proposed solutions was eugenics, the improvement of humanity through selective breeding.

Viewing society as a social organism was another inference from biology. Social evolution was considered by a number of sociologists as similar to biological evolution. Modern societies appeared to be more complex and advanced than primitive societies. The biological analogy was evidenced in comparisons of the "normal body" with the "normal" society (Blackmar, 1915). Social pathology was defined as defects or abnormalities of the interrelated parts of society. The task of sociology was to study these pathologies in order to determine their causes and their cures.

Diversity of definitions has been a continuing anomaly of the social pathology paradigm. The views of Stuart Queen, a longtime advocate of the concept, are illustrative. In an early textbook he considered social pathology as the study of personal and social disorganization (Queen and Mann, 1925). Criticisms of the disorganization perspective led to a redefinition: social pathology as the study of obstacles to social participation (Queen and Gruener, 1945).

Dissatisfactions with the social pathology perspective reached their peak about 1935–1945. Among the most sweeping indictments of social pathology (and related concepts) was an article by C. Wright Mills, soon to become a distinguished figure in sociology. According to Mills (1943), social pathologists were guided by ideologies, beliefs based on their personal origins. Drawn largely from middle-class, Protestant, and rural backgrounds, their norms and values permeated their analyses. The consequence was a piecemeal, unsystematic, atheoretical and conservative opposition to urbanism, heterogeneity, and major social change, particularly of dominant institutions.

These criticisms have diminished, but not halted, interest in social pathology. Renewed efforts have been made to achieve more systematic, objective, and scientific procedures. One influential contribution was made by Edwin Lemert in 1951. Lemert attempted to develop precise criteria for specifying "sociopathic," or pathological, behavior. His efforts, however, have led mainly to the "labeling" view of deviant behavior. That topic will be discussed in a later section.

A more recent attempt to apply the pathology paradigm has urged the use of comparative analysis (Kavolis, 1969). In this view, cross-cultural and cross-historical study of human societies can provide universal criteria of pathology. Rather than relying upon the values and beliefs of any specific group, "destructive behavior" (pathology) would be based on the "implications of the major ethical systems of mankind" (1969:3). What these universal values may be, or how they could be explored and applied, was not explained.

The Disorganization Paradigm

Although "social disorganization" was most widely used between the 1920s and the 1940s, the term is traceable to an earlier era. Charles Horton Cooley, a major contributor to sociology and social psychology, considered social organization to be the unity of relationship between the individual and society. As he put it, "Self and society are twin-born" (1909:5). For Cooley, the dominance of outdated, traditional, ritualized, or bureaucratic practices was "too much mechanism" in society, or "formalism." Unfortunately, this feature of his concern with the problems of social organization has been ignored.

Formalism, "mechanism supreme," was conceived of as the logical source of disorganization, "mechanism going to pieces" (1909:347–349). Cooley contended that formalism produced rigidity, routine, boredom, apathy, and intolerance. The outcome was disorganization, the disintegration of society, of cooperation, of moral unity. Describing "the later centuries of the Roman Empire, when its system was most rigid," Cooley wrote, "the people become unpatriotic, disorderly, and sensual" (349). Though his values were showing most clearly, his concern with disorganization helped to set the stage for its later acceptance.

More detailed and systematic usage of the concept was stimulated by an important research contribution. In their classic study, *The Polish Peasant in Europe and America* (1918–1921; revised 1929), William I. Thomas and Florian Znaniecki offered a modified definition of social disorganization. Rejecting the absolute standards of judgment used by many of their predecessors, they proposed a more relativistic criterion.

Social disorganization, according to Thomas and Znaniecki, referred to "a decrease of the influence of existing social rules of behavior upon the individual members of the group" (1929:II, 1128). Personal judgments, the rules of other societies, and "diagnoses" of abnormality were excluded from consideration. Rather, the breakdown of a group's customs, traditions, and laws was the hallmark of the condition.

Somewhat parallel was their concern with *personal disorganization,* "a decrease of the individual's ability to organize his whole life for the efficient, progressive, and continuous realization of his continuous interests" (1929:II, 1128–1129). Here too the definition is relative, based on the individual's "continuous interests" rather than upon some absolute standard of abnormality or pathology.

Their definitions of social and personal disorganization were adopted widely, often without considering their implications or shortcomings. Applications were made to a variety of groups and conditions: Community disorganization was linked to delinquency and crime; family disorganization, to desertion, divorce, and infidelity. Although the assessments of the concept and its usage have been rather unfavorable, the basic aspects of the paradigm have not been wholly abandoned.

Certain premises of the social disorganization paradigm were examined critically by C. Wright Mills in the article on social pathologists cited earlier (1943). Mills considered the proponents of both perspectives to have been influenced by middle-class, Protestant, and rural ideologies. The social-disorganization stress on "breakdown of rules" placed traditional values and rules beyond examination or questioning.

By implication, the modern, changing, heterogeneous society is disorganized; the immobile, rigid, even stagnating society is not disorganized. In the modern society composed of diverse religious, political, economic, and racial groups with opposing interests and values, whose standards are "the existing rules"? Thus, change and diversity are equated with social disorganization, while traditionalism and conformity are the apparent solution.

Mills' comparison of *cultural lag* with social disorganization is illuminating. William F. Ogburn introduced this term in a book entitled *Social Change* (1922). To Ogburn, *material culture* (technology, transportation, housing, and so on) changes readily. The needed adaptations to these changes in *non-material culture* (rules, customs, laws, and so on) change more slowly and unequally. The gap between them is cultural lag.

The social-disorganization focus upon breakdown of rules is oriented ideologically to the past, particularly to rural values of stability and tradition. The cultural-lag focus upon gaps between material and non-material culture is oriented ideologically to the present, particularly to industrial-commercial values of production and utilization. To Mills, value judgments underlie and permeate both interpretations.

The Value-Conflict Paradigm

An important source of the value-conflict paradigm, according to its founders, was a 1925 article by Lawrence K. Frank. In it, he suggested that social problems arise from failures of existing social institutions and cultural traditions—an interpretation contrary to the social disorganization "breakdown of rules." Frank pointed out that housing shortages, infant mortality, and industrial conflict were traceable to the carry-over of outdated values and practices. Solutions to social problems required the reconstruction of culture and the creation of new designs for living.

Drawing upon Frank's views, and the criticisms of then prevalent usage, Richard C. Fuller (1938) proposed a new and very influential view of social problems. Fuller saw values as central to social problems in three ways: (1) as the basis of what is considered undesirable, e.g., poverty or theft; (2) as the cause of undesirable behavior, e.g., "pecuniary values" encourage theft; (3) as the basis of disagreements over solutions, e.g., punishment versus rehabilitation.

In his 1938 article Fuller described social problems with a statement that has been widely accepted as its essential definition. "They represent a social condition which is regarded by a considerable number of individuals as undesirable, and hence these persons believe that something 'ought to be done' about the situation" (419). This statement, however, referred *only* to the first of his three references to the relevance of values.

Some sociologists who have adopted this public opinion (as I have called it) definition have tended to ignore his other concerns with values. To Fuller, the *objective* aspect of a social problem refers to the actual condition, such as crimes or unemployment. The causes of the objective condition were attributed to the values of the group, his second point noted above.

The distinction between objective and subjective aspects of a social problem was made by Fuller and Myers in 1941. The objective condition, they asserted, was a "verifiable condition which can be checked as to existence and magnitude by impartial and trained observers" (1941:320). The *subjective* element referred to the awareness by people that a condition is "a threat to certain cherished values."

As an illustration of the importance of the subjective element, Fuller and Myers cited the objective condition of racial discrimination. Given the beliefs and values of most southerners, however, racial discrimination was not a social problem in that region. *"Social problems are what people think they are"* (1941:320; their italics). They did not point out that, by their definition, the advocacy of racial equality in the South was a social problem.

Another important aspect of Fuller's value-conflict perspective was the place of values in solutions to social problems. His views on this third point were detailed in an earlier article: "Since in dealing with social problems we are in the realm of values and not the laboratory of the natural scientist, solutions do not follow from analysis of causes. . . . For this latter element [solutions] in the discussion of social problems it is indeed doubtful that there can ever be a scientific frame of reference" (1937:500).

Faith in people appears to have been Fuller and Myers' premise about solutions. As they saw it, "every social problem has a natural history" (1941:320) passing through the stages of "awareness, policy determination, and reform" (321). Becoming aware of an undesirable condition leads to discussion and controversy over what is to be done. The outcome is reform. In other words, solutions are the natural consequences of group awareness. Unrecognized conditions are "latent, dormant, or potential problems" (328).

The latter aspect of the value-conflict paradigm has been emphasized by a noted contemporary theorist, Robert K. Merton. In his words, "Apart from the manifest social problems—those objective conditions identified by problem-definers as at odds with social values—are latent social problems, conditions that are also at odds with values current in the society but are not generally recognized as being so. The sociologist does not impose his values upon others when he undertakes to supply knowledge about latent social problems" (Merton, 1971:806).

Criticizing Fuller and Myers' statement that social problems are what people think they are, Merton has suggested that sociologists should *not* limit their inquiries to recognized, that is, manifest, social problems. When the public is unaware of conditions contrary to their values, it is the task of sociologists to identify and study these latent social problems. An important implication of Merton's view is that the public conceptions may err in overlooking or underestimating an undesirable condition—that is, one contrary to their values. Another possibility not considered by Merton is that the public may imagine or exaggerate the undesirability of some objective condition—that is, one which is not contrary to their values.

A basic assumption of the value-conflict paradigm, specifically noted by Merton, is that it does not rely on the personal values of the sociologist. By defining social problems as the conflict between values or between values and conditions, the sociologist "does not impose his values." True enough. It is obvious that the values of the group are the basic criteria of social problems for this paradigm.

Like other sciences, sociology is said to be neutral and value-free. Later, evidence concerning the value assumptions and implications of modern science will be considered. For the present, it is pertinent to note that the value-conflict viewpoint merely replaces the personal values of the sociologist with the values of a majority or large numbers of people. This substitution of values is not a neutral position for sociology.

The Deviance Paradigm

The central focus of the deviance paradigm is the undesirable behavior of individuals. A number of other terms have been used in somewhat similar ways. Defective, inferior, maladjusted, disorganized, and abnormal people or behavior are among the conceptual predecessors and parallels to deviance. Specific topics have included paupers and criminals, homosexuals and the mentally ill, delinquency and alcoholism.

Low intelligence, lack of ability, and aggressive instincts were among the early explanations of deviant behavior. More commonly, social influences have been emphasized. Currently, sociologists are much concerned with the ways certain kinds of behavior come to be viewed as deviant by members of the society.

The study of crime and delinquency has been a major source of the deviance approach. One important influence has been the *differential association* theory developed by the well-known criminologist Edwin H. Sutherland. First proposed in the early 1930s, the theory has been amplified in the many revisions of his widely used textbook *Criminology* (Sutherland and Cressey, 1970).

According to Sutherland, criminal behavior is learned, like other forms of behavior, through close association of individuals with others. This learning includes attitudes toward the law and techniques for committing crime. Boys who grow up in areas where delinquency is widespread will learn to become delinquent; in other areas, they will not.

Some proponents of the differential association theory have linked it to the concept of "anomie." In 1897, Emile Durkheim, an influential French sociologist, had sought to explain why suicide rates varied from group to group while remaining rather constant within each group. One factor was anomie, the lack of regulation by society of the unlimited wants and aspirations of the individual. Durkheim contended that anomie, or normlessness, when characteristic of society, led to personal dissatisfaction and despair. Suicide could be expected to occur more often in such a setting (Durkheim, 1951).

In a much cited article, "Social Structure and Anomie," Robert K. Merton (1938) used American society to illustrate his use of the conception. Merton, whom I mentioned earlier, noted the emphasis on monetary success in the United States. At the same time, there are many barriers, such as poverty and racial prejudice. The discrepancy between the dominant goal of success and the barriers to real opportunity promotes "the strains of anomie." The outcome is apt to be some form of deviant behavior.

The concepts of differential association and anomie (among others) have been used as social explanations of deviance. Another concern of sociologists has been the nature and the influence of the "label" convict, neurotic, or "queer" upon the individual. We turn next to this *labeling* aspect of deviant behavior.

Edwin M. Lemert, also mentioned earlier, has been a key contributor to the labeling, or *societal reaction*, perspective. In his book on *Social Pathology* (1951), Lemert suggested that the reaction of the group to deviant behavior often tended to strengthen rather than to reduce it. For example, prisons seem more effective in producing "hardened" criminals than in reforming them.

Whatever the original causes of deviant behavior or *primary deviation*, the social penalties result in *secondary deviation*. This condition refers to the new roles, self-images, and rationalizations that characterize the confirmed deviant. In the words of the old saying, "Give a dog a bad name and he'll live up to it," the labeling theory views social stigma as a largely unintended indoctrination for the career of deviation.

Recognition of the influences of labeling has led to exploration of the ways by which certain kinds of behavior come to be defined as deviant by society. Howard Becker, a leading contributor to labeling theory, has examined the role of *moral entrepreneurs* (1963). These are the rule creators and rule enforcers of the society. Legislators, psychiatrists, moral crusaders, and prosecutors are in the business, so to speak, of defining and controlling undesirable behavior.

In an article entitled "Whose Side Are We On?" (1967), Becker discussed the difficulties of avoiding value judgments in studying deviants. To Becker, the *hierarchy of credibility* means the popular tendency to accept the perceptions and moral positions of those at the top of the social structure. Sociologists who adopt the views of superordinate groups narrow their vision and understanding. Those who pay attention to the views of the deviant, however, may face charges of bias and irresponsibility.

Critics of the labeling perspective have contended that it tends to neglect the actual harmfulness of certain forms of deviance. By emphasizing the influence of stigma, the "sociology of the underdog" relieves the deviant from responsibility for his action (Schur, 1971). The view of deviant as victim places blame on society and its dominant groups.

A related criticism is that labeling theory oversimplifies the causes of deviation. Some advocates of this perspective seem to say that the labels—mental illness or criminal—are the basic causes of the behavior (Scheff, 1966). The critics contend, however, that the causes of primary deviation lie not in the labeling process itself but in a variety of other social conditions, such as conflict or poverty (Gove, 1970).

The central premises of the deviance paradigm have built upon, and moved beyond, its predecessors. From the pathology paradigm has been derived a concern with abnormal behavior and the notion of societal defects. To the social disorganization paradigm is owed the "breakdown of rules" conception. The value-conflict paradigm's distinction between objective condition and subjective definitions, as well as its focus upon values, has also been influential. Our next section will consider some implications of the labeling view of deviance by examining the influence of public opinion on social problems.

The Multiple Paradigms of Social Problems

A central feature of scientific paradigms, for Kuhn (1970), has been their tendency to persist for long periods of time, as long as centuries. Our prior sections on social problems paradigms revealed major changes after a decade or two. Moreover, older perspectives have not died or faded away. Rather, they seem to live on, with greater or lesser modification. Some social problems textbooks continue to use all or most of those which we have reviewed (Rubington and Weinberg, 1971; Horton and Leslie, 1974).

Unlike the natural sciences, the social sciences are characterized by the coexistence of many competing paradigms (Lowry, 1974). Multiple paradigms remain characteristic of social problems analysis. Innovations not only produce new paradigms but are also adopted and adapted by prevailing paradigms. As new concepts emerge, older ones may be revised, and accepted assumptions can be sustained under the cloak of changed terminology.

The social problems paradigms we have considered have accepted, in varying ways, a common basic premise, namely, that social problems are identified from the perspective of society's beliefs, norms, and values. Before examining the implications of this assumption, let us view its relationship to the other approaches.

The social pathology paradigm has been the least explicitly dependent on the beliefs and values of society. Its advocates contended that they were relinquishing the moralistic judgments of their predecessors. As Mills disclosed, however, social pathologists were guided by middle-class, rural, Protestant ideas and preferences. The recent advocacy of comparative study has expanded the scope of social pathology to cross-cultural value systems. Whether limited to a class or enlarged to many societies, public beliefs and values have infused the pathology paradigm.

As we have seen, emphasis upon a breakdown of societal rules is central to the social disorganization paradigm. Determining these rules requires data concerning the beliefs and values of the members of the society. Advocates of the paradigm did not clearly specify whether the accepted norms were those of a simple majority or of any large number of people. In either case, some conception of public opinion is the criterion of norms and of social disorganization.

Public opinion is clearly the criterion of the Fuller-Myers statement of the value-conflict approach to social problems. As they saw it, social problems are what people think they are. Merton's reference to latent social problems focused upon the discrepancy between people's values and objective conditions. Public preferences are the standard for identifying social problems. The role of the sociologist is to reveal unrecognized social problems.

The deviance paradigm also rests upon public opinion, since deviant behavior refers to violations of the rules, laws, and values of the group. The concept of labeling refers to the process by which individuals are designated and stigmatized for their socially disapproved characteristics and actions. Although the labeling theorists have raised questions about its basis and its consequences, they have not provided any alternative standards for improving societal judgments.

The Public Opinion Paradigm

Our prior discussion has shown that the accepted paradigms have tended to share a common premise. Explicitly or implicitly, they have conceived of social problems from the perspective of the group's beliefs and opinions, norms and values. I have chosen to call this perspective, its assumptions and implications, the public opinion paradigm. In my view, it is a more inclusive, dominant, or master paradigm of social problems. Differences between the others are mainly paradigm variations.

My intention in describing the public opinion paradigm in this section is critical as well as explanatory. By specifying its basic characteristics, I hope to clarify its shortcomings more precisely. My goal is to formulate a more justifiable, alternative perspective.

As we have noted, recognition of the reliance on public opinion as a definer of social problems is not new. Exponents of the various paradigms have stated, sometimes quite explicitly, their acceptance of this premise. Awareness of its shortcomings, however, has been less explicit or when specified, promptly ignored (see, for example, Merton, 1971:801; Dentler, 1971:14–15) by the advocates. A number of recent textbooks, however, have been sharply critical (Perrucci and Pilisuk, 1971; Sykes, 1971; Gliner, 1973; Henslin and Reynolds, 1973; Freeman and Jones, 1973; Skolnick and Currie, 1973).

Before examining the criticisms, let us review the practical and theoretical utility of the paradigm. First, public opinion seems an appropriate criterion for social problems in a democratic society. Second, public opinion provides an alternative to personal judgments by the sociologist. Third, it provides a source of information from many people—very necessary to the often ivory-towered sociologist. Fourth, and most important theoretically, knowledge of public conceptions of what is undesirable helps sociologists to understand and predict societal responses to these conditions. For these reasons, public opinion provides necessary, though insufficient and at times even erroneous, data about social problems.

The useful aspects of the public opinion paradigm need to be retained. The shortcomings or anomalies suggest the need for revision. First, the views of significant numbers of a majority are inappropriate standards for a hetero-geneous, multigroup society. Second, the beliefs and val-ues of group members are inappropriate criteria for a supposedly neutral or value-free sociology. Third, influ-ences of powerful groups, such as government, corpora-tions, labor unions, and the mass media, on public opinion are given implicit endorsement. Fourth, the paradigm fails to provide any basis for excluding erroneous, exag-gerated, or doubtful public judgments of what is undesir-able. Fifth, objective conditions are subordinated to subjective interpretations as criteria of social problems. Sixth, if social problems are undesirable conditions, are they "solved" by changing beliefs and values?

Growing awareness of the anomalies is illustrated by the comments of a leading contributor to the public opin-ion paradigm. In an article entitled "Social Problems" in the prestigious *International Encyclopedia of the Social Sciences,* Lemert states: "This definition more or less identifies sociologists with the lay populace and makes public opinion sociological opinion with implied faith in the democratic process. Its difficulties accrue from recog-nition of the irrational or spurious qualities in public ex-pressions of collective behavior...." (1968:454). The question is, what are the alternatives?

Some Questions and Answers

A major justification of the public opinion paradigm has been its presumed objectivity and neutrality. That is to say, the personal beliefs and values of the sociological observer are excluded as definitions of social problems. Replacing the judgments of sociologists with those of the public—whether a majority or large numbers of people—does not produce a value-free definition. The outcome is a substitution of one set of values for another, not their elimination.

Several related questions emerge. Can values be eliminated? If not, whose values will be used? Why should one set of values be chosen in preference to any or all other values? Can values be evaluated? If so, how?

The answer to the first question, to a growing number of sociologists, is negative. To them, and I agree, values cannot be excluded from the study of social problems. "There has yet to be any extended analysis of social problems which did not contain an army of value judgments in its arguments—and this is inevitable. Value judgments are inherent in the subject-matter; as Arthur Miller said in *Death of a Salesman,* they 'come with the territory.' And it is best to grapple explicitly with that which cannot be avoided" (Sykes, 1971:21).

A similar view is held by Perrucci and Pilisuk (1971:xviii): "The definition of a social problem reflects the norms and values of the definer." Whose values should be used? Accepting the tenet that science cannot make value judgments, they propose their own specifically value-oriented criteria for identifying social problems: These values include life, dignity, resources, freedom, and responsibility. Conditions adverse to these values are social problems.

Reliance upon the value commitments of each individual sociologist is an explicit alternative to those of the public. The outcome, however, would be scientific anarchy—disorderly disagreements over personal preferences. Why should *you* accept *my* unsupported choices? Unless I can suggest some justifiable rationale, there is no reason why my personal choices are "better" than anyone else's.

The comparative approach to values, noted earlier (Kavolis, 1969), is a possible answer to our questions. By studying other societies, Kavolis believes that we can find the common values shared by humanity. This procedure is more reasonable than accepting the standards of any individual or any single society. I believe that such comparisons would broaden the base of our value judgments.

Still, it is doubtful that the diversity of communist-capitalist, democratic-totalitarian, militarist-peaceable, Christian-Buddhist-atheist-etc. societies can produce universally acceptable value systems.

We have arrived at the final, the ultimate questions. Can values be evaluated and, if so, how? The answers are crucial to the study of social problems. We have seen that definitions of social problems require value judgments. We are told that science is neutral and value-free. If our premises are correct, we are faced with an apparently paradoxical conclusion: No definition of a social problem is scientifically justifiable.

The conclusion is logical; the resulting choices are limited. One possibility, accepting the conclusion, offers only unsatisfactory options. We can continue to study social problems while debating forever the question of values. Or, to be scientifically neutral, we must expel the concept of social problems from the sociological vocabulary.

There is another possibility. The conclusion assumes that the premises are correct. Do definitions of social problems require value judgments? The evidence, some already discussed, clearly supports an affirmative answer. Is science neutral and value-free? Here the answer is less clear-cut. Many scientists assert that it *is*. Others contend, and offer substantial evidence, that it is *not*.

In forthcoming sections, I shall review the evidence that values are central to science. Furthermore, I shall consider the applicability of these values, particularly the value of knowledge, to the study of social problems. Specifically, I propose to use the knowledge and values of science as a paradigm for social problems.

Toward a Knowledge-Values Paradigm

Let us begin our discussion of the proposed paradigm by considering the relevance of knowledge for the study of social problems. Knowledge is the very essence of science. The term science comes from the Latin *scientia*—knowledge. To require that social problems be defined by sociologists in accordance with scientific knowledge may seem self-evident.

The public opinion paradigm subordinates scientific knowledge in favor of the beliefs of significant numbers of people. That the public may fail to recognize the existence of "undesirable conditions" has been pointed out by Merton (1971:806). Latent social problems is his term for these unrecognized conditions. In this case, sociological knowledge is considered superior to public lack of knowledge.

In the past, and to some extent today, people believed in the existence and the harmfulness of witches. According to the public opinion definition, witches were, and perhaps are, a social problem. "Is the sociologist who joins the search for witches, their causes, and consequences, a neutral observer or a participant in witch-hunting?" (Manis, 1974a:309). The public opinion paradigm doesn't distinguish between facts and myths, between spurious and real social problems.

The case for knowledge as a basis for defining and studying social problems can be concluded with a more current example. Marihuana is strongly feared and opposed by many millions of Americans. Legal penalties have been severe. Convicted users have received lengthy jail terms, as much as twenty years. "The public position seems to be based on many erroneous beliefs: that it is addictive; that it is debilitating; that it invariably leads to other addictions; that users are sexually depraved" (Manis, 1974b:4). Experts disagree (see Goode, 1969; Grupp, 1971).

Since people are opposed to marihuana, its usage may be considered a social problem from the public opinion perspective. Since great numbers of people believe it undesirable, presumably it is an important social problem.

Such opposition based on erroneous beliefs is a poor substitute for judgments based on factual knowledge. We have seen that the public opinion paradigm is not value-free. At times, it is apt to be knowledge-free.

That definitions of social problems should be based on accurate knowledge needs little additional discussion. We need only point out that science provides research and theoretical techniques for acquiring demonstrable knowledge. Facts are the undisputed province of science. The place of values is said to be somewhere else—religion, morality, tradition, or personal choice.

We need not question the relevance of values for the behavior of the individual. Our actions are influenced by our likes and dislikes, by our beliefs about what is good and what is bad. Values permeate our conscience and influence our reasoning. The statement "Don't give me any facts, my mind is made up" may reflect a closed mind and/or unchangeable value preferences.

We need not question the relevance of values for society and its institutions. The term ethnocentrism refers to the tendency of members to accept the beliefs and values of their society and to use them as standards for judging others. Traditional values make up much of our social heritage.

Social institutions, organizations, and interest groups may hold similar or conflicting values. These include the various religions, families, political parties, corporations, and labor unions. We are aware of their values and accept their efforts to promote those values. Yet, some people, including scientists, do not realize that the scientific establishment has become a major force in the modern world.

Science is a basic institution of contemporary, industrialized societies. Like other institutions, it is guided by certain value premises. As we have seen, scientists may not be fully aware of these influences upon themselves and upon society. The belief that science is neutral is contrary to our present-day knowledge about science.

The relationship of science to values will receive more

attention in the following chapter. Now, it must suffice to point out that individual scientists and their organizations are becoming concerned. The question of values is a prime interest of the *Bulletin of the Atomic Scientists* and the British Society for Social Responsibility in Science. Values, ethics, and morality have been themes of sessions of the American Academy for the Advancement of Science and of the professional associations of physicists, biologists, psychologists, and sociologists.

Before proceeding any further, I shall state the definition of social problems that will serve as the basis for the knowledge-values paradigm. *Social problems are those social conditions identified by scientific inquiry and values as detrimental to human well-being.* Later sections will explain this definition, its implications, and its relationship to public conceptions of undesirable conditions.

Beyond Freedom and Dignity?

The preceding discussions may suggest a frightening prospect. Scientific knowledge and values have been proposed as criteria for determining the existence of social problems. A corollary is that the values and knowledge of science will be good for humanity. Since science "knows best," should science be empowered to control human behavior? Some, ignoring the limitations of science, say it should.

In *Beyond Freedom and Dignity* (1972), the eminent psychologist B. F. Skinner advocates the scientific control of all human behavior. He contends that our "terrifying problems" are the products of the outdated myths of freedom and dignity, myths that conceal the actual control of behavior by "contingencies of reinforcement," the environmental determinants of our actions. Skinner proposes that unplanned, harmful conditioning be replaced by scientifically designed "schedules of reinforcement."

Skinner is convinced that the science of human behavior is sufficiently advanced to justify such control. He appears to believe (though, as a behaviorist, he doesn't believe in beliefs!) that his proposals will persuade people to give up their (imaginary!) freedom and dignity. The apparent remedy for problems is a benevolent oligarchy —Big Brothers in the white coats of science.

There are many reasons for rejecting such a proposal. We need only discuss the nature of science to reveal the shortcomings of Skinner's position. Our discussion also will seek to clarify the intended usage of the knowledge-values paradigm.

Science is only one of many human activities and institutions. The knowledge and values of science differ from those of the arts and the humanities, such as literature, music, and painting. They differ, though perhaps in lesser degree, from those involved in family life, democratic governments, and the ethical systems of religion. Skinner advocates scientific dominance. The knowledge-values paradigm is intended for sociological analysis of social problems. Informing society of sociological interpretations permits a "real-world" examination of their accuracy and utility.

Science is guided by interpretations—concepts, theories, and paradigms that, at times, have been misguided or erroneous. The social sciences, far less advanced than physics and chemistry, are marked by mistakes and controversy. The changing paradigms of social problems reveal uncertainties in sociology. Skinner would impose on society a psychological perspective based mainly on researches with rats, guinea pigs, and chickens. The knowledge-values paradigm is intended as a spur to further research and a potential source of suggestions for social action.

The individual sciences are abstract and one-sided. It has been said that the scientist is someone who knows more and more about less and less. Scientific specialization can bring about an "ivory-tower" isolation and produce barriers to communication even among scientists. Few scientists are trained to "put it all together." For example, critics have noted Skinner's limited understanding of economics, political science, and sociology. Narrow oversimplifications by the knowledge-values paradigm will require careful examination.

The practice of science is careful, methodical, and slow. Human behavior is, and often must be, spontaneous and quick. Policy-makers do not have time to wait until all the facts are known. Indeed, it is unlikely that the largest or most complicated computer will ever be able, or be permitted, to store all the information about everyone and everything. Skinner's scientist-rulers are more apt to be rulers than scientists. The knowledge-values paradigm is more appropriate for an informed people than for an omniscient elite.

To summarize, the knowledge-values paradigm is *not* designed to serve as a blueprint for dictatorial social engineers. Rather, it is intended to provide an appropriate—that is, scientific—perspective for sociological analysis. It is more suitable than the prevailing paradigms. Before attempting to explain and apply it, we shall examine more thoroughly the place of facts and values in science.

Summary

Scientific paradigms are the accepted ways of conceiving the subject matter of a scientific specialty. The study of social problems is characterized by multiple paradigms: social pathology, social disorganization, value-conflict, and deviance. Whatever their differences, however, sociologists usually define social problems as whatever many people think they are.

I have called this common viewpoint the public opinion paradigm. An important anomaly of the paradigm is that it may be applied to trivial or even imaginary conditions.

Another anomaly is the possible neglect of genuinely harmful conditions. For these reasons, I define social problems as those social conditions identified by scientific knowledge and values as detrimental to human well-being.

In Chapter 2, I shall explain my rationale for using scientific knowledge-values to identify social problems. My thesis is that science offers more appropriate criteria for sociological analyses than those based on popular beliefs. That science can provide a factual basis for interpretation of phenomena is seldom questioned. Still, many doubt that science can formulate or justify value standards. After examining the relationship between facts and values, I shall discuss some specific knowledge-values of science and their relevance for studying social problems.

RECOMMENDED READING

Conant, James B. *On Understanding Science.* New York: Mentor Books, 1951. A paperback written with clarity for non-scientists. Very good on the development and the role of modern science.

Fuller, Richard C. "Sociological Theory and Social Problems." *Social Forces* 15 (May 1937): 496–502. An early article from which the value-conflict paradigm was developed.

Kuhn, Thomas S. *The Structure of Scientific Revolutions,* 2nd ed. Chicago: University of Chicago Press, 1970. This book helps to explain the importance of scientific paradigms and the reasons why they are accepted or replaced.

Lemert, Edwin M. *Social Pathology.* New York: McGraw-Hill, 1951. Despite the title, the book introduced some of the basic ideas of the labeling approach to deviance.

Lippmann, Walter. *Public Opinion.* New York: Macmillan, 1922. The first chapter of this classic study by a distinguished journalist-philosopher is excellent.

Lowry, Ritchie P. *Social Problems.* Lexington, Mass.: D. C. Heath, 1974. A comprehensive discussion of popular myths and scientific paradigms concerning social problems.

Lynd, Robert S. *Knowledge for What.* Princeton: Princeton University Press, 1939. A classic work by an eminent contributor to sociology. Chapters on "Values and the Social Sciences" and "Some Outrageous Hypotheses" are especially worthwhile.

Manis, Jerome G. "The Concept of Social Problems: Vox Populi and Sociological Analysis." *Social Problems* 21, no. 3 (1974): 305–315. A critique of the public opinion approach to social problems, with criticisms of the value-free assumption.

Merton, Robert K. "Social Problems and Sociological Theory." In *Contemporary Social Problems,* ed. by Robert K. Merton and Robert Nisbet, pp. 793–845. New York: Harcourt Brace Jovanovich, 1971. A leading contemporary theorist includes an explanation of latent social problems in a strong case for social definitions of social problems.

Mills, C. Wright. "The Professional Ideology of Social Pathologists." *American Journal of Sociology* 49 (September 1943): 165–180. The study of social problems owes much to this sweeping critique from the soon-to-be notable sociologist.

———. *The Sociological Imagination.* New York: Oxford University Press, 1959. Opposing "grand theory" and "abstracted empiricism," Mills advocates study of the social structures that impede solutions to social problems.

Reynolds, Paul D. *A Primer in Theory Construction.* Indianapolis: Bobbs-Merrill, 1971. Chapter 2 of this brief book contains descriptions and examples of paradigms in the social sciences.

Seeley, John R. "The Making and Taking of Problems: Toward an Ethical Stance." *Social Problems* 14 (Spring 1967): 382–389. This fine article discusses some of the "nonsense" and the omissions of current definitions of social problems. The author suggests the need for an ethical stance by sociology.

Skinner, B. F. *Beyond Freedom and Dignity.* New York: Bantam Books, 1971. The leader of the "operant-conditioning" school of psychology explains how "a technology of behavior" can solve our problems.

2
Facts and Values

"Facts are facts and values are values and never the twain shall meet." This thought has comforted generations of theologians, philosophers, and scientists. There are important differences between facts and values, and I shall deal with them. My aim will be to locate their possible meeting place, particularly with reference to social problems.

The traditional view has been that facts (and similar terms) are a part of science, while values (and similar terms) belong to religion and philosophy. Stated briefly, *facts* refer to "what is"; *values* refer to "what ought to be." Science is said to describe and explain hard reality, while philosophy and religion provide justifications for ideals, ethics, and morality.

This division of labor between science and philosophy/religion is a basic premise of the public opinion paradigm of social problems. The earlier discussion of the value-conflict conception considered "objective" and "subjective" aspects of social problems. The objective element is the "verifiable condition" that science investigates. The subjective element includes the values that provide "solutions." The latter were said to be beyond scientific inquiry. My criticism is that the division of labor is based, in part, upon an outdated understanding of modern science and philosophy.

Historians are agreed that the beginnings of modern science took place during the seventeenth and eighteenth centuries. Prior to that period, explanations of nature and of humanity were offered by religion and philosophy. Some of these explanations ran counter to the changing conditions of the times: growing populations, larger cities, more commerce, increased travel, the spread of Protestantism, the development of capitalism, and new discoveries and inventions.

· Many innovations were accepted readily; some were not. Improvements in glassmaking led to knowledge about magnifying and the invention of the telescope. Navigators, generals, and astronomers quickly adopted the telescope. The observations of astronomy, however, led to controversial conclusions. Galileo's data confirmed that the earth was a planet rotating around the sun. Charged with heresy by the Catholic Church, Galileo recanted. Still, his findings and those of others could not be suppressed.

We need not be concerned with the causes of the new climate of ideas or the specific discoveries (see Whitehead, 1948; Merton, 1970). We are concerned with the gradual concession, by philosophers and theologians, of observed facts to the new sciences. The concessions were slow, often reluctant, but they were made. The outcome was an uneasy compromise. The compromise is important for the study of social problems.

An Uneasy Compromise

A short summary of the compromise requires that we compress and simplify the divergent views of many people over several centuries. The outcome itself is rather clear—the emergence of supposedly neutral, value-free science. Briefly, this dominant viewpoint or paradigm was a product of the early successes and struggles for recognition by science. In general, the domain of science was considered limited to the factual observations guided by "rational" methods. The common goal is "objective" knowledge.

By comparison, the arts (or the humanities) were to deal with "subjective" knowledge. These usually include the fine arts, such as literature, music, and painting, along with philosophy and religion, ethics, faith, values, and the like. The modern college of arts and sciences is a product of this division of knowledge.

The general compromise included a variety of unstable, lesser compromises. In the past social philosophy included economics, sociology, and political science. Today, they are considered to be social sciences. History is still viewed by many as part of the arts or humanities, while psychology is often located in a college or division of the sciences.

One of the influential justifications for this division of knowledge was proposed by the eighteenth-century British philosopher David Hume. According to a recent writer, "The source of the separation of fact statements and value statements is David Hume's famous rule which asserted that since both statements belong in different categories, the latter cannot be deduced from the former" (Walter, 1970:119).

Hume contended that facts were determined by reasoning or rationality. Morals, preferences, and values were said to be based on the "passions" (emotion). Thus, reasoning and evaluation are logically separate processes. What is true or false cannot explain our judgments of good or bad, of likes and dislikes.

The division between facts and values was incorporated in John Stuart Mill's authoritative *A System of Logic*

(1843). "Propositions of science assert a matter of fact: an existence, a co-existence, a succession, or a resemblance. The propositions now spoken of do not assert that anything is, but enjoin or recommend that something should be. They are a class by themselves. . . . [These are] the Art of Life, in its three departments, Morality, Prudence or Policy, and Aesthetics" (1947:619–620).

Despite the differences between the "is" and the "should be," Mill saw two important relationships between them. He asserted that achieving desired goals could be aided by the facts and logic of science. That is, science can provide the means by which the ends of the Art of Life can be reached. Mill was convinced, also, that a basic principle or standard of human behavior could be established. He suggested that promotion of happiness be considered as the ultimate goal or value of humanity.

The pursuit of happiness was a basic feature of the doctrine of utilitarianism. To its proponents—Mill, Jeremy Bentham, and others—human behavior appeared to be motivated by the seeking of pleasure and the avoidance of pain. Therefore, the utility of social practices and institutions could be determined by their consequences for human happiness. "The greatest good for the greatest number of people" was the general principle of the utilitarians. Policies for achieving this goal could be reached best by representative government.

Critics rejected the premise that happiness is the ultimate goal or value of humanity. They opposed the equating of morality with pleasure, of goodness with happiness. They said that the sources of individual happiness included such incompatible actions as generosity and miserliness, power and submission. For some, knowledge is enjoyable, while for others, "ignorance is bliss." Above all, argued some opponents, utilitarianism derived questionable values from dubious facts.

Disagreements over the relationships between facts and values have not ended. Still, despite the criticisms of the utilitarian position, its premises or their parallels have permeated modern interpretations of social phenomena. In economics, the public good is one rationale for limiting supposedly free competition. In psychology, the pleasure-pain assumption underlies the theories of conditioning and reinforcement. In sociology, the values of significant numbers of people have been the criteria of social problems. Despite these value premises, the social sciences are said to be neutral and value-free.

Knowledge and Ideology

During the Middle Ages in Western Europe, religion was the authority for all knowledge. Beliefs about God, nature, and humanity were decided by official proclamation. Theology was the arbitrator of knowledge. Although disputes with royalty or with heretics occurred, the dominant influence on the knowledge of the era was the social institution of the Church.

The development of modern science brought into question some of the accepted beliefs, the presumed knowledge. Discoveries by the new astronomy, physics, chemistry, and biology gradually weakened the religious monopoly on knowledge. One consequence was a scientific monopoly on empirical, factual knowledge.

Religious values were also being shaken. For many centuries, the Church had opposed "unjust profit," usury, and even commerce itself. The sin of avarice was the basis for the dictum "No Christian ought to be a merchant" (Heilbroner, 1953:16). To the Catholic Church, capitalism was a growing problem.

Despite the opposition of the Church, commerce expanded greatly. The expansion was aided by, and contributed to, the growth of cities, improved technology, changes in economic theories, and the spread of Protestantism. In the following section, I shall review some of the forces that changed the image of capitalism from a harmful to a desirable condition. Our purpose is understanding the social basis of factual and evaluative knowledge.

Certain ideas of Karl Marx are especially relevant to our concerns, not only his interpretations of capitalism, but also those views that led to the sociology of knowledge. To Marx, "modes" of subsistence and production in each society determined the nature of social relationships. Thus, feudalism was based on the ownership of agricultural lands. The lord of the manor owned the land and controlled his serfs or peasants. Obedience to aristocracy and the "Divine Right" of kings were accepted beliefs and moral obligations (Marx and Engels, 1947).

Changes in the modes of production were claimed by Marx to have resulted in the decline of feudalism. The economic basis of society was transformed by improvements in technology—tools, instruments, ships, printing, weapons, and so on. New modes of production resulted in new classes—from peasantry to proletariat, from aristocracy to bourgeoisie—and the new business class had new beliefs and values such as free trade, supply and demand, equal rights, and shared political power.

Each era was said to be guided by its ideologies, ideas generated by the "material conditions" of its time. Thus, to Marx, the beliefs and ethics of the bourgeoisie were ideologies that grew out of their class position and therefore were often justifications for their class interests.

Marx's conception of ideology has been described as total rather than particular. That is, he did not limit the idea of ideology to specific beliefs of individuals but to the basic foundations of entire thought systems (Mannheim, 1936). While conceding that various circumstances might affect specific individuals, Marx stressed that beliefs and preferences were social products of their time and place.

A frequent criticism of the Marxist thesis is its disregard for the importance of traditions, faiths, and convictions. Not only critical of these ideologies, Marx also did not consider them to be as influential as economic conditions. An eminent contributor to sociology, Max Weber is among those who have held differing interpretations. First published in 1904, his *The Protestant Ethic and the Spirit of Capitalism* (Weber, 1958) was focused on the influence of a religious value system.

Why was capitalism as a comprehensive economic system adopted in Western civilization and not elsewhere? Why were some European peoples more receptive to capitalism than others? Weber asserted that differences in religious ethics were the explanation. Protestantism, and particularly its ascetic denominations—such as Calvinism, Methodism, and Puritanism offered a code of ethics that fostered capitalism.

From the sermons, speeches, pamphlets, and books of these denominations, Weber extracted the relevant ethical ideals—the virtues of prudence, diligence, honesty, and thrift. As Methodist leader John Wesley put it, "We ought not to prevent people from being diligent and frugal; *we must exhort all Christians to gain all they can, and to save all they can; that is, in effect grow rich*" (Weber, 1958:175). Conversely, such behavior as idleness, pleasure, and spending were deemed undesirable, even sinful.

The emerging Protestant ethics, according to Weber, differed greatly from Catholic ethics. For the former, wealth was not a sin but evidence of "divine providence." Business was not immoral and undesirable but a "calling." The outcome was a moral climate favorable to economic development, to the spirit of capitalism. The undesirable conditions or problems of the Middle Ages became the desired values and goals of the Age of Commerce.

Ethical Neutrality?

Weber was concerned with the influence of ethical beliefs upon the social sciences as well as religion. Several essays on the former topic, written between 1903 and 1917, have been published in English in *The Methodology of the Social Sciences* (Weber, 1949). In them, Weber agreed that the study of value judgments and their influences could be conducted scientifically, although he was strongly opposed to the acceptance or espousal of values by scientists and teachers.

Difficulties were recognized. "Nor need I discuss further whether the distinction between statements of fact and value-judgments is 'difficult' to make. It is" (1949:9). Still, the effort must be made, since "ethical neutrality" is required of scientific inquiry. Science is empirical, not normative. It can describe and explain; it cannot tell us what is good or bad.

Weber admitted that the choice of topics for study by sociologists and economists is guided by personal preferences and values. He recognized "the fact that in social sciences the stimulus to the posing of scientific problems is in actuality always given by *practical* 'questions'" (1949:61). These remarks have been interpreted to mean that personal or social values may promote scientific investigation but should not influence observation and analysis.

For Weber, the ultimate values and purposes of mankind are beyond scientific explanation or justification. Sociology can reveal the objective facts required to achieve social values and the factual consequences of those values. Like other sciences, sociology portrays the "is"—the "should be" is beyond its scientific limits.

Weber's conception of the ethical neutrality of science, based on the distinction between facts and values, has been an important rationale for a value-free sociology. It has benefited sociology by encouraging objectivity, by revealing the influences of bias, by improving research techniques, and by raising the stature of the field. It has also been a justification of the public opinion paradigm of social problems as a substitute for the sociologist's personal values.

For the study of social problems, the value-free perspective has created scientific problems. Since social problems include both objective conditions (facts) and subjective judgments (values), sociologists have been impeded in their efforts to make sense of the topic. As one writer has described the situation, "... no coherent scheme of classification, analysis, prediction, and control of contemporary social problems is possible" (Dentler, 1971:7). Given the assumption of ethical neutrality, the conclusion appears appropriate.

A major implication of the value-free perspective is sociological neutralism toward all norms and values. If a society advocates peace or war, headhunting or witch-hunting, women's liberation or white supremacy, none can be considered social problems. Sociology can describe and explain their characteristics, their causes, and their consequences. Sociology cannot evaluate the conditions or the consequences, according to the value-free position.

In the words of a critic, "I contend that Weber's thesis necessarily leads to the view that every preference, however evil, base, or insane, has to be judged before the tribunal of reason to be as legitimate as any other preference" (Strauss, 1963:425). As we have seen, Weber's position is based upon a distinction between facts and value. Both can be studied, but value judgments are excluded from science.

The case for scientific neutrality rests upon certain assumptions that need to be examined closely, It is based on a logical contradiction. Another critic has made this point, writing that "... for science the word 'ought' ought never to be used, except in saying that it ought never be used" (Lynd, 1948:181). That is, science *should be* neutral.

More important is the factual assumption that the progress of science is a result of its value-neutrality. The Weber position is that science is, as well as should be, neutral. Let us turn next to evidence of the place of values in scientific development.

"Pure" Science

Whatever the controversies over the scope and methods of science, many scientists appear to agree on its basic goal—the attainment of demonstrable knowledge. The value of knowledge for its own sake is often considered as sufficient justification for science. Even values themselves —once excluded from science—are open to scientific scrutiny. Oddly, factual knowledge about the motives, norms, values, and institution of *science* is recent and sparse.

Philosophers, psychologists, political scientists, and sociologists have begun concerted studies of science. Much of the history of science has been unassisted by the tools, concepts, and theories of the social sciences. Often, conjecture and unstated value judgments have been merged with empirical data.

Explanations of the earliest origins of science are an appropriate place to begin. "Science seems to have come into existence merely for its bearings on practical life" (Sullivan, 1949:7). (Note the *merely*.) What is the "scientific spirit"? It is "disinterested curiosity in the workings of nature" (1949:9). Not solutions to practical problems but disinterested curiosity is the approved motivation in this view of "pure science." Still, the emergence of science is generally conceded to have been a response to group needs and values.

Leaping to seventeenth-century England and the records of its Royal academy, we find pure and applied science to have been about equally important. According to Robert K. Merton's tabulation of the academy's research discussions, "it appears that less than half (41.3%) of the various investigations conducted during the four years in hand were devoted to pure science" (1970:203). Most of the not-so-pure investigations were aimed at solving the practical problems of naval transport, military technology, manufacturing, and mining. The interests and values of government, commerce, and the military were served by the reported experiments.

During the seventeenth century, "England attained its position of military and commercial leadership" (1970:184), a position achieved in large part by technology based on applied research. Likewise, the external values of commerce and government had influenced the scientific enterprise. While Puritan values also were influential, I shall discuss those influences in a later section. For the present, I shall examine some assumptions and consequences of the scientific enterprise.

An eminent scientist has asserted that, in the past, "those investigating the structure of the universe imagined themselves as the equivalent of the early explorers and map makers" (Conant, 1953:93). Conant described their beliefs as fallacies, misconceptions based on a mistaken analogy.

According to him, "the analogy between the map maker and the scientist is false. A scientific theory is not even the first approximation to a map; it is not a creed; it is a policy—an economical and fruitful guide to action by scientific investigators" (1953:97). Science does not only attempt to describe what is, but more important tells researchers what to do. Most important from the standpoint of society, these theory-policies tell us all what to do, what to believe, and what to value.

Scientific concepts, theories, and paradigms guide researchers toward valued, significant knowledge. Sociologists ignored poverty for decades because it did not seem important. Classical economists have been concerned with supply and demand because the presumed law is important. Marxist economists have other explanations and criteria (see Lynd, 1948:183).

Knowledge as Power

The knowledge-seeking policies of science have transformed not only science but also nature and society. The pure sciences have not only observed what is but also have altered and created phenomena. New chemicals, atoms, forces, and social relationships are among their many consequences. Nuclear fission, antibiotics, fertilizers, defoliants, behavior modification, and monetary policies are products of science. Describing the activities of nuclear physicists, molecular biologists, oncologists, and criminologists as neutral and value-free is erroneous.

Knowledge is power. It cannot be neutral. Nor has it been. Those who control knowledge—church, state, military, or science itself—control society and, increasingly, nature. Knowledge can be sought and used for war or peace, wealth or poverty, medicine or machines, pollutants or purifiers. What we explore or create will be determined by value judgments. Who makes these judgments, and on what criteria, are critical concerns for science and for humanity.

"If, for example, cloning (the duplication of genetically identical individuals from the cells of a complex, multicellular living organism) were achieved in human beings, what effect would this have upon the traditional concept of identity? What 'super-race' or society of acquiescent servants might arbitrarily be produced by those in power" (Mann, 1970:1). Today, such questions are neither farfetched nor rare.

A recent writer on science policies has said that ". . . the works of science are the symbol of the twentieth century, in the same way that Pyramids are the symbol of Pharaonic Egypt, the cathedrals the symbols of the Middle Ages or the Palace of Versailles the symbol of the age of Louis XIV. . . ." (Salomon, 1973:65–66). We have mentioned only a few of these products. We need to know how the policies of science are determined.

However science is defined, the number of professional scientists is small, but the consequences of their policies far exceeds their numbers. A national register of American scientists listed only about 313,000 in 1970 (National

Science Foundation, 1971). About 40 percent were employed in education, 31 percent by industry, and 10 percent by government.

Government policies extend far beyond the actual employment of scientists. Most university funds for research are obtained by grants and contracts from various governmental agencies. During the 1960s, about half of all research and development expenditures in the leading Western nations was made by their governments (Blume, 1974:21). In the United States, the federal proportion has approached two-thirds of all funding. Political policies are a crucial source of the policies of contemporary science.

That modern science is "inherently political" (Haberer, 1969:2) is the conclusion of studies by historians, political scientists, and sociologists. The tools, techniques, and facilities of research are increasingly expensive. As a consequence, the activities of pure and applied science are guided by those who hold the purse-strings. Though knowledge is a basis of power, so too political and economic power control the search for knowledge (Greenberg, 1967:270ff).

Industry and commerce continue to influence science. The employment by business of scientists is needed to create the products of public consumption. Social sciences also serve the marketplace by developing the techniques of persuasion to stimulate public demand. One of the big buyers is government. Through military and space programs, government indirectly purchases the services of science. Billions of dollars are allocated for industrial contracts that guide the search for, and the applications of, scientific knowledge.

These forces have been reviewed in a recent history of American science. The final words of the study are a prediction based on current conditions. "What is likely is that it [science] will lose the last vestiges of its autonomy, and that the conditions for the pursuit of science will change even more profoundly in the next decade than they have in the past" (Daniels, 1971:344).

The influence of expanding science is very great. What knowledge is sought and how it is used are crucial issues of our time. What is defined as socially desirable or undesirable will guide the scientific enterprise. What part science itself will play in these decisions is important for society as well as for science.

The Sociology of Knowledge

Beliefs that modern science is neutral or guided mainly by disinterested curiosity are incomplete and misleading. The individual scientist may be motivated by the search for knowledge for its own sake. Professional recognition is still another personal motivation. However, in addition to these individual influences, we must also examine the social influences upon scientific knowledge.

According to Karl Mannheim, one of its founders, the *sociology of knowledge* deals with the social basis of all knowledge (1936:237ff). In his words, individuals "do not confront the objects of the world from the abstract levels of a contemplating mind as such, nor do they do so exclusively as solitary beings. On the contrary, they act with and against each other in diversely organized groups, and while doing so they think with and against one another" (1936:3).

Knowledge was considered by Mannheim to be influenced by its societal context. Thus, the ideas of truth and goodness in the medieval era were interpretations based on the dominance of the Church. More broadly, language and traditions mold the forms of knowledge. Ideas about what is and the desires for what should be are shaped by society.

Within each society, group membership and social position influence individual "perspectives" (1936:244). Social classes and occupational groups observing the same situation see things differently. The thoughts, concepts, and judgments of the observer are social, as well as individual, products.

Studying these social influences upon scientific knowledge is a concern of the sociology of science. During the past few decades, sociologists have begun to explore the ways in which scientific activities and knowledge are shaped by society (Barber, 1952; Kaplan, 1964). Their studies show that the search for scientific knowledge is an organized activity of modern society. Usually, scientific knowledge is sought within large-scale, complex organizations, such as universities, corporations, and government. Scientific activities are carried on in accordance with the aims, policies, and resources of these organizations.

Teaching is the primary social role for many scientists. An educational function of science is to train potential entrants into the profession. Often more common is the communication of scientific knowledge as part of a liberal education or as preparation for other professions. Through these activities, existing knowledge of science is disseminated throughout society.

One of the basic conflicts in academic life is that between teaching and research. Although university scientists spend much of their time on teaching, their reputations and their promotions depend upon their publication. Usually, ". . . even in the university, for many people, research outweighs teaching as a source of career commitment" (Krohn, 1971:69). The values of innovation versus dissemination of knowledge are sources of scientific tensions.

The roles of scientists in industry and government are guided by the specific purposes of their employers. The value aims of the Defense Department define the kinds of knowledge sought by their scientists. Those employed by the electronics, petroleum, or pharmaceutical companies seek otherwise appropriate knowledge. Under those circumstances, applied rather than "pure" knowledge is the expected outcome.

In a broad sense, science has become a major social institution. Like other institutions, science is concerned with its purposes, responsibilities, and values. These concerns are evident in the assertion that ". . . the meetings of the American Association for the Advancement of Science have been distraught for the last four or five years with debates over the social and moral duties of science" (Cattell, 1972:xii–xiii). Before discussing these so-called social and moral duties, I shall review the current position of the fact-value dichotomy.

The Evaluation of Facts

Our consideration of facts and values has relied upon a traditional, simple distinction between them. Historically, facts have been said to be "what is," while values referred to "what ought to be." For contemporary philosophy and science, the definitions are oversimplifications.

Fact statements are beliefs based on the "best" available evidence. There is no guarantee that all the evidence is known. The pursuit of scientific knowledge is a continuous process. "The attainment of settled beliefs is a progressive matter; there is no belief so settled as not to be exposed to further inquiry" (Dewey, 1938:8).

Observation is not a neutral, mechanical process. What we see and hear are influenced by existing conditions *and* by our eyes, ears, and minds. So too are the instruments of science. Ideas and values direct our observations and their interpretations.

The evaluation of presumed facts is a basic task of scientific inquiry. Scientists are frequently faced with the necessity of judging current data. At times the evidence may appear self-contradictory. Conant has pointed out that ". . . in regard to light, however, we can hardly do *better*

than say that light is in a sense both undulatory and cor-
puscular" (1953:71; my italics).

Facts are assessed by the research techniques of scientists. Modern techniques are considered to be more accurate and more precise than older ones. Scientific
instruments and measuring devices are standards or
norms for interpreting phenomena. A norm is a rule for
behavior. Approved rules for exploration and measurement require scientific value judgments.

*"A fact, therefore, is a fact by virtue of its fundamental
value significance"* (Hartman, 1967:219). The significance of facts is evaluated on the basis of their relationship
to theory, as well as the quality of research methods. By
theory is meant a set of related propositions or hypotheses. For example, the kinetic theory of gases includes
statements about molecules, energy, and the relationships
between them.

Preferred theories are those that meet scientific criteria
(Nagel, 1961:90ff.). A good theory is based on specific,
precisely defined concepts. The theory suggests ways of
linking concepts with observations; that is, a theory tells
the researcher what to look for and how to do it. The
standards are sometimes called "rules of correspondence." Finally, the relationship between concepts or
propositions should be logical and not contradictory, as
well as testable. These technical norms are important elements of scientific values.

Scientific paradigms are broad sets of ideas that guide
the search for facts and theories. What is defined as fact
or theory is guided by these broad viewpoints. Some scientists make little distinction between theories and paradigms. Examples include the wave theory of light and the
social disorganization theory of social problems.

New paradigms emerge in science when traditional
ones are found wanting. However, interpretations that
appear contradictory, doubtful, or unsupported by research are not easily replaced. The history of science is

marked by numerous instances of resistance to new ideas (Conant, 1951). Beliefs in the existence of phlogiston, in the caloric theory of heat, and in nature's "abhorrence of a vacuum" led to many erroneous conclusions.

The retention or change of paradigms is influenced not only by belief and evidence but also by value assumptions. Evolutionism was, and is, opposed because of its moral implications. To Darwin, survival of the fittest was the source of evolutionary change. Both survival and fitness are evaluative as well as descriptive terms (Pepper, 1970). They assume that living organisms are impelled by natural purposes and that natural selection requires a continuous struggle for survival. These interpretations of facts involved value judgments.

From Facts to Values

The most persistent argument for the exclusivity of facts and values has been that values cannot be derived from facts. Describing "what is" cannot tell us "what ought to be." Therefore, we are told, the scientific search for knowledge cannot, and should not, be a guide for human purposes. Although there are many unresolved, critical issues, modern science and philosophy have begun to question these traditional assumptions.

A long-established claim has been that ethics and morality are part of religion and philosophy. Facts and theories are part of science. As we have seen, the search for scientific knowledge involves evaluation and interpretation as well as observation. Neither religion nor philosophy ignore facts. As one noted philosopher puts it, "I would not give the least credence to an *ought* which did not come out of an *is*" (Pepper, 1947:81). At a minimum, facts must be known as a means for achieving personal values and ethical goals.

Knowledge is a value. Acquiring knowledge requires

observation, evidence, and theory. The goal of good health can be achieved by knowledge of the usefulness of antibiotics, nutrition, sanitation, and physical exercise. Knowing that smoking can lead to lung cancer provides one criterion for choosing between the values of health and relaxation at work and the appearance of sophistication.

Another traditional contention is that facts are objective and neutral, while values are subjective and personal. The Romans had a phrase for it, *de gustibus non disputandem est.* That is to say, matters of taste are unarguable. Certainly, for many individuals, preferences and purposes are resistant to change or discussion. It is paradoxical that the frequent fact of value-subjectivity is used as an argument for the inevitability, if not the desirability, of value-subjectivity.

We have seen that the search for facts is often guided by values. Likewise, the study of values can be based on facts. This study is not limited to religion or philosophy. Values, norms, and ethical practices are studied by social sciences. They are no more subjective and personal than motives, opinions, attitudes, customs, or political party preferences. Like them, values are a factual subject matter of economics, psychology, and sociology.

"Value thus is no more, and no less, arbitrary or subjective than is fact" (Hartman, 1967:129). The quotation is from a book on axiology, the scientific theory of values. By studying what values are, we can learn how they are acquired, how they may be achieved, and what their consequences might be. Such knowledge is needed for choosing between different values.

A traditional view holds that values are essentially emotional. Facts are said to be rational. From this position, scientific knowledge is based on reasoning and logic. What is considered good or bad, moral or immoral, evil or ethical is said to be non-logical, even irrational. Therefore, goes the argument, logic and reason cannot be used to decide what is basically non-logical and emotional—human values.

This distinction, like the others, has some merit. Reason *is* different from emotion. Also different are night and day, work and play, male and female. Shall we say, merely, *viva la difference?* We need not and should not. Both reason and emotion can be observed as facts of human behavior. We know fairly well how to recognize and judge rationality. We can identify emotions and feelings. We are beginning their evaluation.

Some emotions are demonstrably harmful to the individual and to society. Unrealistic fears are characteristic of certain neuroses and psychoses. Feelings of hostility can lead to bloody feuds, riots, and wars. Conversely, "tender, loving care" is recommended as an emotional condition for "good" child-rearing. Emotional maturity involves feelings of respect and tolerance. These interpretations combine, sometimes only implicitly, facts and values. They may be considered as efforts to apply rational evaluation to emotions and feelings.

Lastly, I shall examine a scientific justification for denying that values are derivable from facts. To social scientists, values are learned from society. The culture of a society includes values from its religions, traditions, and social practices. Since cultures differ, there are no universal values. Moreover, within each society, competing groups differ in their goals and moral preferences. For these reasons, we cannot expect value consensus among people.

Knowledge of facts is claimed to be different. Though interpretations of reality may change, scientists believe that there are underlying laws of nature. Theories are viewed as successive approximations to more accurate knowledge. The value of demonstrable knowledge to science is the basis of its codes of ethics. Since other people and cultures have different values, their conduct cannot be judged by scientific standards. In short, science is universal, while values are relativistic.

This traditional viewpoint is being challenged. Some scientists have questioned whether the purpose of science is knowledge for its own sake. A number of nuclear physicists and molecular biologists, for example, have become concerned over the social responsibility of science. They have asked that science place the value of human survival, safety, and well-being above the value of knowledge itself.

There appears to be a growing number of philosophers who doubt the "absolute" relativism of values. As we have seen earlier, they are examining facts as means to achieving values and also values as facts. They assert that such study can lead to greater understanding and agreement on values. "Indeed, there can be no question as to whether observation and scientific knowledge is relevant for determining the answers to ethical questions" (Brandt, 1959:37).

Determining these answers will not be easy, to put it most mildly. Strong arguments for distinguishing facts from values should not be ignored. The "is" differs from the "ought to be." However, we must consider also the implications of their relationships.

The answers to fact-value questions are especially important for definitions of social problems. Prevailing definitions, using public opinion and values, are based on a traditional conception of science. Popular preferences as criteria of social problems are neither neutral nor, any longer, scientifically justifiable.

Public Opinion and Scientific Knowledge

I have proposed that scientific knowledge and values be used in defining social problems. In this section, I shall attempt to explain and justify the relevance of scientific knowledge. The next section will present my suggestions for the use of scientific values.

Public opinion and scientific knowledge are not mutually exclusive. Although public opinion is affected by tradition, leadership, and advertising, the data and theories of science also permeate modern societies. Mass media and mass education spread information about important research findings.

Influences of public opinion upon the social sciences are not uncommon. In sociology, public opinion has been the standard for defining social problems. Group preferences for democracy and free enterprise are reflected in the paradigms of political science and economics.

These comments are not intended to imply that public opinion is always incorrect, nor that scientific knowledge is always correct. Both change. However, scientific knowledge is guided by specialized techniques aimed at testing interpretations. The cross-national character of science reduces the biases of specific cultures.

The complexities of modern society require the advancement of knowledge. Technology, communication, organizations, and economic policies depend upon informed people. Democracies are especially dependent upon a knowledgeable electorate. Solving social problems can be facilitated by encouraging inquiry and spreading knowledge.

The diffusion of scientific interpretations is the strongest test of their accuracy. Knowledge can be compared with traditional beliefs and with the claims of propagandists. Widespread knowledge can be an effective weapon by society against manipulation by the elites of government, of business, and of science itself.

A major feature of advanced nations is the predominant usage of scientific knowledge for commercial, military, and political purposes. Lesser effort has been expended to obtain and disseminate knowledge relevant for protection of the environment, delivery of health care services, or solving the problems of alcoholism, mental disorder, or divorce.

If knowledge is power, a monopoly on knowledge is a form of concentration of power. As Woodrow Wilson once said, "What I fear most is a government of experts. God forgive that in a democratic society we should resign the task and give the government over to experts. What are we for if we are to be taken care of by a small number of gentlemen who are the only men who understand the job? Because if we don't understand the job, then we are not a free people" (cited in Lapp, 1965:1).

Scientists are increasingly aware of the dangers of monopolized knowledge. Some see an emergent "science establishment" linked with and serving big government and big business (see Greenberg, 1967:Ch. I). The question "What is science for?" (Dixon, 1973) is important to science and to society.

Such questions involve the value assumptions of science. Traditionally, scientists have espoused the search for knowledge for its own intrinsic value. Increasingly, they find knowledge serving the goals of militarism, power, and profit. This trend requires reexamination of the values of science.

Deciding what science is, or is supposed to be, involves beliefs and values. My conception of science has been described briefly by a theoretical physicist: *"Science is Public Knowledge"* (Ziman, 1968:8). In this view, science is not only a method or a private body of knowledge. It is not merely a collection of disciplines, nor is it restricted only to experts. It is also a vital aspect of modern culture.

Scientific knowledge is advanced by amateurs and by professionals. It is created and spread by teachers and students, used in colleges, industry, and government. It is a growing element in public opinion. Bridging the gap between erroneous belief and substantiated evidence is a major task of science and of society.

The Values of Science

Scientists have devoted much attention to their methods of observation and interpretation. Less attention has been paid, in the past, to their values. They have tended to assume that science is "disinterested curiosity" aimed at accumulating verifiable knowledge. That assumption is no longer self-evident.

Recent decades have seen an expanding examination of the basic values of science. As a consequence, we now know a great deal more about the scientific enterprise. There appears to be substantial consensus that science should aim at rationally verifiable and transnational or universal knowledge. There is general agreement that scientific knowledge should be shared. There is also acceptance that such goals require individual freedom to explore and to disagree.

Certain reservations concerning these values are being voiced. Should science seek knowledge that might destroy humanity—which includes scientists? Nuclear physicists have opposed the search for knowledge of more destructive atomic weapons. Biologists see great dangers to humanity in certain areas of virus and bacterial research. Concern for the ethical use of human subjects in research is increasing.

These issues involve the social responsibility of science. They are especially relevant for the traditional norm of scientific neutrality, the assumption that science is value-free and "disinterested." Recent researches suggest that the belief in scientific objectivity is unwarranted (Mitroff, 1974:587). Some scientists assert that *commitment* to theories and to values is necessary for science.

Given these different views, can scientific values offer guidance in defining and solving social problems? I believe they can and should. Scientific values are more consensual than those of diverse groups and societies. They are linked to factual knowledge of nature, human beings, and culture. They are congruent with the needs of modern life. Like scientific knowledge, they are open to continual scrutiny and discussion.

Proposing scientific knowledge-values as criteria for judging social conditions does not require their imposition on society. Science is one of many societal activities. All that is proposed here is the open sharing of scientific knowledge and values with society.

Before specifying these knowledge-values, let me review my conception of science. I noted in Chapter 1 that the root meaning of science is knowledge. Considered as public knowledge, science is a contemporary cultural process (Richter, 1972). Like other aspects of culture, science is learned, communicated, and changeable.

By cultural process, I mean that science is a continuing activity of modern societies. A noted anthropologist preferred to call this process *sciencing* rather than science (White, 1949:Ch.1). The verb sciencing focuses on the ongoing behavior of people. Specifically, sciencing is a systematic way of interpreting, explaining, and dealing with the physical and social world.

Science offers a way of knowing. I have contended that this behavior is not neutral, value-free, or passive. It involves observation of what is and the creation of what has never existed in the past. It involves judgments over what is worth knowing and what is worth seeking.

A study of the sociology of science portrays "science as a moral enterprise" (Barber, 1952:93). In the past, the moral premises of science were taken for granted. No longer. As we have seen, the value standards of our scientific endeavors are a growing concern of science and society.

For the present, the exploration of scientific values is in its infancy. Still, we can draw upon the ideas and data of a growing number of investigators. We are also free to make our own suggestions and criticisms. My own interpretations of scientific knowledge-values are not expected to be conclusive. Like others, they are open to questioning and replacement. The contemporary study of values by science and philosophy will lead to "better" answers.

My intention is to clarify the knowledge-values of science in order to guide our study of social problems. Such criteria are more suitable for scientific purposes than those of large numbers of people or individual preferences. My specific criteria are related to the conception of science as a cultural process aimed at improved public knowledge.

In succeeding sections, I shall discuss three categories of knowledge-values appropriate for contemporary science. First are intrinsic values, those most directly related to knowledge. Second are contextual values, those required for knowledge from society. Third are social responsibility values, those involving the obligations of knowledge seekers to society.

These are somewhat overlapping provisional statements. The categories need careful appraisal and cautious application. Their order of presentation does not imply any rank order of priorities. The inevitable tension between these values will be apparent as we try to apply them. From such reality testing, we can advance our understanding of social problems.

Intrinsic Values

The value of knowledge is central to science. "Pure" scientists view knowledge as the only goal of science. For them, the only scientific norms are those involved in seeking and accumulating knowledge. I have chosen to call these approved norms or rules of knowing, the *intrinsic* values of science.

One of the intrinsic values of science is *empirical* knowledge. That is scientific conclusions are supposed to be based on demonstrable evidence. Among the approved ways of obtaining empirical data are observation and experimentation. The test of knowledge lies in the research process.

By contrast, popular beliefs are derived from a variety of sources. They may be influenced by research findings. Or, they may originate in emotion, propaganda, rumor, or tradition. For example, some ideas about blacks ("lazy") and homosexuals ("crazy") are empirically unwarranted. Knowledge of these ideas helps to explain the behavior of those who hold them. To scientists and others who value empirical knowledge, however, the unsupported beliefs are not justifiable.

Another intrinsic value is *theoretical* knowledge, which includes hypotheses, generalizations, and other abstract propositions. Such statements may be derived from empirical findings. Conversely, theoretical propositions can be used to predict empirical outcomes.

An illustration is the theory of differential association. As we saw in Chapter 1, the theory aims to analyze and explain criminal behavior. It was based, in part, on observed data. It is also congruent with the more general propositions about human socialization.

Although theoretical knowledge may appear to resemble ordinary beliefs, scientists stress the importance of empirical verification of their interpretations. Furthermore, theoretical and empirical knowledge are subject to continuing appraisal. Scientific knowledge is always open to criticism, revision, and replacement. My proposed knowledge-values paradigm for social problems is only one of numerous proposed alterations in knowledge.

There is an old tale of two scientists who passed some sheep in a nearby field. One scientist remarked to the other, "Those sheep seem to have been shorn recently." The other replied, "At least on our side." Humorous or not, the story exemplifies another intrinsic value of science—*organized skepticism* (Merton, 1973:277).

Scientists assume that knowledge is advanced through careful scrutiny and interpretation. Even the seemingly obvious cannot be taken for granted. An open mind, curiosity, and critical judgment are required for scientific knowledge.

Another intrinsic value of science is called *universalism.* Knowledge has no boundaries of nationality, class, race, sex, or age. Research findings should be judged on their merits, not by the characteristics of the researcher. Violations of universalistic standards do occur. At times, individual scholars may be blinded by personal prejudices, ethnocentrism, or nationalism. Scientists may be reluctant to give up long-established theories or paradigms. National or cultural preferences are especially common biases in the social sciences. Whatever the difficulties, universal criteria are valued by science.

Like the other intrinsic values, scientists advocate universalism because of its suitability for knowledge. "Science is universal by nature: the truths which scientists pursue are not national truths; they are the same everywhere, and therefore can be universally recognized" (Salomon, 1973:209).

These intrinsic values of science are standards for judging the quality of knowledge. They can be used to appraise beliefs about nature and about human beings. They are applicable to the study of social problems. They can help us distinguish genuinely harmful conditions from imaginary or exaggerated ones.

Contextual Values

The search for knowledge cannot be isolated from its social context. Like other human activities, knowledge-seeking is influenced by group conditions. As noted earlier, seventeenth-century science was stimulated by commerce, religion, and government. Nazi scientists were required to endorse the idea of Aryan superiority. Military policies have played an important part in guiding scientific inquiry. The social milieu of science is an important concern to us.

The *contextual* values of science are the desirable societal conditions conducive to the intrinsic values of science. In order to seek empirical and theoretical knowledge, scientists must not be restricted by custom or power. They must be free to ask questions and to doubt conventional beliefs. National, cultural, or racial barriers to knowledge are contrary to the intrinsic value of universalism.

Freedom of inquiry is one of the basic contextual values of science. Researchers need to be kept immune from political, religious, or other public pressures. Achieving accurate data requires independent, unhampered opportunity of thought and action.

Societies that impose a variety of restraints on knowledge are antagonistic to the goals of science. In the Soviet Union, the rights of researchers are controlled by communist political leadership. Although the social sciences have been controlled more than the other sciences, even agronomy and chemistry have been controlled arbitrarily. Such restrictions are incompatible with the value of free inquiry.

A related contextual value is *freedom of expression.* The accumulation of knowledge requires opportunities for communication. Free speech, correspondence, and publication are important forms of scientific expression. New theories, research techniques, and empirical data must be disseminated in order to be used. An open society facilitates the dissemination and improvement of our knowledge.

Science depends upon a wide latitude of free expression. National and regional organizations offer public forums for presenting ideas and findings. Specialized publications are sources of comparison and inspiration. Through public discussion, errors and misconceptions are corrected. The outcome is improved knowledge.

The costs of science must not be overlooked. The pursuit of knowledge is expensive and time-consuming. Most applicable to the natural sciences, increasing costs are becoming characteristic of the other sciences. Science cannot be continued without such societal investments. The *support of inquiry* is another contextual value.

To promote the search for knowledge, modern societies spend large sums of money on scientific training. Equipment for observation and analysis—laboratories, instruments, records, and computers—is expensive. Research projects require qualified personnel as well as appropriate suppliers.

Support of inquiry is not restricted to research grants. Like other people, scientists need food, shelter, clothing, medical care, and so on. The achievements of the scientific enterprise depend upon societal support and protection. Science does not exist in a social vacuum. The contextual values of science refer to the requirements from society by those who seek knowledge.

The pursuit of knowledge is an activity of many human beings—professional scientists, teachers, students, and others. An obvious prerequisite for this pursuit is the survival of humanity. No people, no knowledge. Hence, preservation of the human environment, by preventing nuclear devastation and the spread of cancer-producing pollutants, is necessary for the *protection of knowledge.*

Less destructive than atomic warfare but more common are the deterioration of our cities, race and sex biases, and societal manipulation by powerful elites. Such conditions, are detrimental to the well-being of humanity and to its search for understanding.

Contextual values are apt to be taken for granted by scientists. They are not self-evident to others. Indeed, there appears to be growing doubts about the desirability of scientific activities. Science itself is perceived as the source of nuclear bombs and dangerous chemicals. It arouses fear of manipulation. It seems threatening to favored beliefs.

A French statesman, Georges Clemenceau, remarked

that war is too important to be entrusted to generals. His comment is applicable to other experts. Knowledge is too important to be left solely to a few scientists.

Knowledge-seeking is not limited to science. Nor are its consequences. Others need to share scientific knowledge. And others are concerned with the effects of science on their lives. These concerns are reflected in expanding economic, legal, and administrative controls upon science.

I have already mentioned the influences of government and commercial funding upon research activities. New federal policies concern the protection of human subjects who participate in experiments. A growing number of scientists are raising questions about these policies. They are also examining their own ethical obligations to humanity.

Social Responsibility Values

I have asserted that the justification for the ethical neutrality of science is no longer self-evident. My reason is the growing number of scientists who are describing their ethical obligations to humanity. The titles of recent books by scientists reflect the concerns: *Reason Awake: Science for Man* (Dubos, 1970); *The Social Responsibility of Science* (Brown, 1971); *Science, Scientists and Society* (Beranek, 1972); *Scientists in Search of Their Conscience* (Michaelis and Harvey, 1973). These volumes are among the many public statements of scientific values.

The recency and diversity of scientific discussions of ethical questions suggest cautious interpretations. Most apparent is the increasing extent of such discussions. The outcome is less clear-cut. Hence, my view of the social responsibility values of science is a tentative one.

An oft-stated social responsibility of science is the *communality of knowledge* (Barber, 1952:92). By communality is meant the obligation to share knowledge with others. Knowledge is not supposed to be private property.

The only approved reward for new knowledge is public recognition.

In the past, communality of knowledge was held to be important solely for science itself. Scientists have long recognized their dependence upon the contributions of their predecessors and their colleagues (Merton, 1973:273). The disclosure of new theories and findings is essential to the improvement of knowledge.

Scientists are expected to reveal their methods and data without reservation. Deception and secrecy are contrary to the scientific ethos. More recently, communality has been extended to wider audiences. Viewing science as public knowledge, some scientists emphasize the obligation to inform non-scientists of their conclusions and concerns. A more knowledgeable society is their aim.

That science should be socially beneficial is another social responsibility value. The term *meliorism* (Barber, 1952:66) is used to describe the moral commitment of science to do good and to avoid harm to humanity. Some scientists assume that knowledge itself is sufficiently helpful, while others contend that the issues of goodness and badness are not scientifically relevant. Although scientists remain divided, an increasing number advocate altruistic standards for their inquiries.

A familiar example are those who have refused to conduct research on nuclear, chemical, and bacterial weapons. Another concern is the ethical treatment of human subjects in experimental research.

Some scientists go further. For them, the social responsibility of science includes the obligation to participate in public policy-making. I shall use the term *activism* to refer to this value.

To scientific activists, the aim of contributing beneficial knowledge is insufficient. Activists contend that existing structures of society prevent the application of desirable knowledge. Many of them have urged their professional associations to take stands on public issues. Among the advocated policies have been restrictions on tests of nuclear bombs, the use of pesticides, and deceptive advertising. Also advocated have been increased support of education, health, family, and community research and services.

The opponents of such views fear that scientists will be diverted from their prime concern—the search for knowledge. Another objection is the possible loss of objectivity and accuracy. The question is whether value commitments will distort observations and conclusions. Still another objection is that, for many topics, our knowledge is inadequate.

The proponents of social responsibility values recognize the possible dangers (see Dubos, 1970:110ff). They point out, however, that all scientists have personal values that may bias their analysis. They recognize the gaps in knowledge and urge public admission of the deficiencies. Still, they contend that the social benefits of a responsible science will outweigh the potential shortcomings.

Disagreements over the social responsibilities of science continue. Yet, it is evident that the traditional conception of a value-free science is no longer taken for granted. As we have seen, scientific policies are influenced by governmental financing, commercial employment, *and* social concerns. I believe the latter are most appropriate, particularly for defining and solving serious social problems.

The Sociological Imagination

How can the knowledge-values of science be applied to the study of social problems? The answer requires consideration of sociological perspectives. Here, as elsewhere, we have no precise, agreed-upon guidelines. Some sociologists concentrate upon the accumulation of factual data. Others prefer the construction of comprehensive theories. Still others seek knowledge as a means for achieving socially beneficial goals.

C. Wright Mills has examined these perspectives in his influential book *The Sociological Imagination* (1961). His views provide broad guidelines for appraising social conditions. In Chapters 3 and 4, I shall consider specific theoretical and research criteria for identifying and assessing social problems.

A basic feature of the sociological imagination is moral commitment. According to Mills, "The values that have been the thread of classic social analysis, I believe, are freedom and reason" (1961:130). As he had stressed earlier, unstated middle-class values permeated the writings of social pathologists. Mills' values of freedom and reason are explicit and scientifically relevant.

The central topic of the sociological imagination is the "intersect," or connection, between individuals and social structure. Mills stressed the relationship between "the personal troubles of milieu" and "the public issues of social structure" (1961:8). He asserted that understanding the situation of an unemployed worker is often dependent upon understanding the economic and political organization of society.

"Intellectual craftsmanship" was considered to be the method of the sociological imagination (1961:195ff). Reasoning and logic are necessary for collecting and classifying data. Also important are personal involvement, familiarity with the ideas of other social scientists and of the humanities, and an open, flexible mind.

The values, subject matter, and methods of the sociological imagination are congruent with the knowledge-values paradigm of social problems. As we have seen, the traditional ideas of ethical neutrality, of the exclusivity of facts and values, and of the public opinion paradigm are no longer wholly justifiable. We need to develop more appropriate conceptions and procedures.

Applying the sociological imagination begins with clear

specification of value commitments. The knowledge-values of science—intrinsic, contextual, and social responsibility—are the proposed criteria for identifying social problems. The applications of these criteria can draw upon available data and theories of sociology. My aim is to distinguish genuine or real social problems from spurious or fictitious ones.

After separating the real from the non-real, the next step is to distinguish important or serious social problems from minor or trivial ones. Modern society is faced with many harmful conditions. The knowledge-values paradigm suggests ways of assessing their seriousness. I will examine the primary and structural conditions that lead to numerous, severe troubles for group members.

There are value pitfalls and data gaps in the sociologist's efforts to identify and assess social problems. Proposals for solving social problems involve even more of both. Sociologists often say that "more research is needed." Reasonable conjectures and hypotheses will have to serve, at least temporarily (Nisbet, 1966:18). They are part of the sociological imagination

Summary

Modern science appears to have achieved a virtual monopoly over factual knowledge. Values, ethics, and morality are considered, usually, to belong within the domains of philosophy and religion. The separation of facts and values is a basis for the presumed ethical neutrality of science. Some sociologists claim to be neutral and value-free when they use public opinion to identify harmful conditions. I have contended, rather, that popular values are more to be knowledge-free than value-free criteria of social problems.

Scientific knowledge is not neutral. Science has become

a powerful social force in the modern world. Contemporary scientists not only observe but create new phenomena. Moreover, military, political, and economic policies guide researchers in their inquiries. Increasingly, the question of their value standards is an important concern of scientists throughout the world.

I have pointed out that values guide the search for facts. What kinds of data are deemed relevant, what methods seem acceptable, and what criteria are used for theorizing —all of these involve scientific value judgments. Our knowledge of facts has relevance, also, for our choices among values. Thus, facts are applicable for appraising values.

The suggested knowledge-values of science have been derived from the observations and proposals of sociologists and other scientists. Most agreed upon are intrinsic values, those directly applicable to the search for knowledge. The contextual values of science refer to the desirable social conditions conducive to the intrinsic values. Most debated are the social responsibility values of science, which involve the obligations of science to humanity. These values provide criteria for sociological judgments about social phenomena.

Identifying social problems is the specific purpose of the next chapter. In it, I shall consider the implications of major sociological theories for the study of social problems. I intend, also, to designate and clarify the various sources of problem identification. My aim is to distinguish real from spurious social problems and, later, to assess their seriousness.

RECOMMENDED READING

Barber, Bernard. *Science and the Social Order*. Glencoe, Ill. Free Press, 1952. One of the early systematic contributions to the sociology of science.

Blume, Stuart S. *Toward a Political Sociology of Science.* New York: Free Press, 1974. A comprehensive description and analysis of the relationship of science to government, professional organizations, society, and values.

Gross, Llewellyn. "Values and Theory of Social Problems." Pp. 383–97 in *Applied Sociology: Opportunities and Problems,* ed. Alvin W. Gouldner and S. M. Miller, New York: Free Press, 1965. This brief article explains why science is responsible for defining social problems.

Hagstrom, Warren. *The Scientific Community.* New York: Basic Books, 1965. A detailed analysis of the organization, norms, and values of a national scientific community.

Handy, Rollo. *Value Theory and the Behavioral Sciences.* Springfield, Ill.: Charles C. Thomas, 1969. This clear and readable book examines the scientific approaches to values. It also summarizes the viewpoints of three influential theorists of values.

Horowitz, Irving L., ed. *The New Sociology.* New York: Oxford University Press, 1965. A collection of essays dedicated to C. Wright Mills. Articles by Horowitz, Notestein, and Rapoport are especially pertinent to this chapter.

Laszlo, Ervin, and James B. Wilbur, eds. *Human Values and Natural Science.* New York: Gordon & Breach, Science Publishers, 1970. Excellent articles, too numerous to cite, deal with science and values.

Marx, Karl, and Engels, Friedrich. *The German Ideology.* New York: International Publishers, 1947. A classic work on the social basis of ideas.

Merton, Robert K. *Science, Technology and Society in Seventeenth Century England.* New York: Howard Fertig, 1970. A major contributor to the sociology of science examines the development and influence of science.

Mills, C. Wright. *The Sociological Imagination.* New York: Grove Press, 1961. The first chapter and the appendix on intellectual craftsmanship are very worthwhile.

Ravetz, Jerome R. *Scientific Knowledge and Its Social Problems.* New York: Oxford University Press, 1971. An attempted synthesis of philosophical, psychological, sociological, and technical issues pertaining to modern science. Very good, too.

Sullivan, J. W. N. *The Limitations of Science.* New York: New American Library, 1949. First published in 1933, this book by a scientist-philosopher-writer presents a traditional view of science. The chapter on the values of science is interesting.

Weber, Max. *The Methodology of the Social Sciences.* Glencoe, Ill.: Free Press, 1949. Three articles written early in this century present the "ethical neutrality" position. Their influence on contemporary sociology is but one reason for reviewing them.

Ziman, J. M. *Public Knowledge.* Cambridge: Cambridge University Press, 1968. A professor of theoretical physics defines science as public knowledge.

3
Identifying
Social Problems

In 1966, a National Academy of Sciences report predicted that, on the basis of then current trends, the depletion of oxygen in the surface waters of the United States will reach a crisis state by the year 2000 (Commoner, 1971:219). By that time, the total amount of organic wastes dumped in our inland lakes and rivers will exceed the total oxygen in those waters. This means that even biodegradable wastes will not be decomposing.

I have no certain information, but I assume that most Americans were not then aware of, or concerned about, the information. If not, the condition was not a social problem—in terms of the public opinion definition. As I noted earlier, a Gallup poll found that the vast majority of Americans believed that long hair for boys was undesirable—a social problem, according to that definition.

Popular concerns need to be compared with the views of trained, knowledgeable people, such as scientists, engineers, and psychotherapists. The preceding examples suggest the importance of examining the reasons for their differences as well as their agreements. In order to determine how social problems are identified, I shall discuss some of the relevant sociological paradigms and research procedures.

I shall begin with a brief summary of a major shift in sociological position, from concern with reform toward relativism. Next, I shall discuss some of the broad paradigms (sometimes called perspectives, theories, or models) held by sociologists. Most widely accepted are symbolic interactionism and functional analysis.

Critics have contended that these perspectives exaggerate the extent of order and stability of social phenomena. Some of them have placed more stress on the importance of power and conflict. Another important development that I shall review is the emergence of the sociology of sociology.

The discussion of the preceding topics will need to be brief, as our primary concern is with social problems. The focus of our discussion will be on their relevance for problem identification.

The final set of sections in this chapter will deal specifically with four sources of problem identification: public opinion, knowledgeable people, sociology, and science. This sequence, in the order of their presentation, reflects their increasing relevance to our topic. In other words, the knowledge-values of sciences are the proposed arbiters for judging and identifying social problems.

From Reform to Relativism

The purpose of this section is to examine the relationship between the broad paradigms of sociology and the criteria used for identifying social problems. These paradigms form a frame of reference for social problems analysis. What sociology is supposed to be influences what sociologists do.

As mentioned earlier, the beginnings of sociology in the United States were reformist in character. To a considerable extent, the study of sociology was the study of undesirable conditions. The founders of sociology gave little thought to definitions and criteria. Social problems were self-evident.

Efforts to become more scientific led sociologists toward research and theory. The early concepts were drawn from biology and evolutionism. Viewing society as an organism provided a language of interpretation—human nature, natural selection, adaptation, symbiosis, and pathology. The pathology paradigm looked for defective, unhealthy individuals and social parts. These were the social problems.

The concept of culture gave new direction to sociology. As folkways and mores differ from society to society, the assessment of undesirable conditions, it was contended, could not be universal or absolute. To Sumner, "The mores can make anything right" (1906:521). Cultural relativism became a postulate of sociology and of social problems analysis.

Social organization was defined as the totality of "rules of behavior" connected together in "harmonious systems" (Thomas and Znaniecki, 1927:I, 32–33). The breakdown or weakening of these norms was social disorganization. The internal harmony or discord of a given society has been the relativist standard.

The value-conflict paradigm extended the relativist position. Its founders, Fuller and Myers, saw no scientific way of evaluating values. They also recognized the diversity of groups in modern society. They concluded that it is the "conflict of values which characterizes social problems" (1941:27). Not the values of the entire society but those of considerable numbers serve to identify undesirable conditions.

Sociological relativism is also evident in the deviance paradigm. Usually, deviance is defined as behavior that fails to conform to important group norms. The labeling perspective goes further in raising questions about ac-

cepted group standards. Discussions of stigma and degradation appear to present the deviant as a victim of social
norms. Neither universal nor societal standards, neither
group nor any other criteria are offered for evaluating
behavior or social phenomena.

The relativist position has made unmistakable contributions to sociology. It has forced reexamination of absolutist
value positions. It has increased appreciation of the diversity of human interests and cultures. It has revealed the
unintended consequences of established norms and practices.

Still, relativism has bequeathed a dubious legacy to us.
Is our gift a greater freedom and flexibility? Or is it normlessness and anarchy? Or some combination? For possible
answers to these questions, let us examine some of the
theoretical paradigms of sociology.

Symbolic Interactionism

The American founders of symbolic interactionism are
usually considered to be Charles Horton Cooley, John
Dewey, and George Herbert Mead. Since Mead's "social
behaviorism" is *the* acknowledged source, his views will
be summarized (Mead, 1934; Meltzer, 1972). Early in this
century, behaviorists opposed the use of such terms as
mind, ideas, and thinking because they were subjective
and unscientific. Mead contended that social behavior
could only be understood and explained with such conceptions.

To Mead, the human infant becomes a social being
through interaction with others. Learning language, the
principal means of communication, makes social relationships possible. Without language, the individual is
scarcely human. Words are not merely sounds or marks
on paper. They are symbols whose meanings are shared
by group members.

The acquisition of symbols by the individual is necessary not only for communication with others but also with oneself. Mead used the term *mind* to refer to this inner process of communication. The *self* referred to the ability of the individual to be an object of action as well as an actor. That is, mind and self permit self-directed behavior and relationships between people.

From this perspective, human actions are not automatic responses to environmental stimuli. Rather, they are an ongoing process of interpretation and direction, or construction, of behavior. To illustrate going to get groceries involves a complex variety of thoughts, choices, and actions—decisions concerning if, when, where, what, and so on to buy.

The view of society as symbolic interaction has had important influences upon social problems analysis. The leading contemporary exponent of symbolic interactionism has been Herbert Blumer (1969), who gave the perspective its name. In one of his influential articles, Blumer has stressed the importance of examining the ways individuals and groups perceive and create their social worlds (1962).

With this in mind, Blumer stated that " . . . social problems are fundamentally products of a process of collective definition instead of existing independently as a set of objective social arrangements with an intrinsic makeup" (1971:29). He pointed out that sociology has found no way of evaluating social conditions. Consequently, sociology must be concerned with collective behavior, the processes by which the group decides what is undesirable.

Blumer asserted that sociologists have tended to ignore this collective process of problem identification. Although they define social problems as conditions deemed undesirable by society, they have not explored how and why people form their opinions. Instead, he claimed, sociologists have concentrated on describing and explaining the supposedly undesirable conditions.

Inspection of social problems textbooks reveals that Blumer's description is accurate. Much attention is given to analyzing "harmful" conditions, much less to public problem-defining. Neglect of the latter topic is a notable deficiency (a recent exception is Mauss, 1975). Limiting the study of social problems to social *issues*, however, diverts attention from the social *conditions*.

Popular conceptions of what is undesirable at times are influenced by emotion rather than knowledge. We do need to know more about such influences. We also need to know more about the actual causes and the consequences of social problems. Above all, we need to be able to distinguish real from imaginary social problems.

Symbolic interactionism can aid in such efforts. For example, it has been a prime source of the labeling approach to deviance. The concept of labeling has focused our attention upon the unanticipated and often unwanted consequences of social definitions of undesirable actions. It has also led to proposals for decriminalizing "crimes without victims," such as homosexuality (Schur, 1965).

Another possible application of symbolic interactionism has been suggested by Jaeger and Selznick (1964:653–669). Viewing culture as a "world of symbols," they urge that evaluation of human symbolizing be a task of the sociology of culture. "A normative theory of culture is a way of taking seriously the idea that culture is an adaptive product, a result of individual and social striving for symbolically meaningful experience" (1964:666).

Such efforts are congruent with the knowledge-values paradigm of social problems. For example, conditions that prevent development of "symbolically meaningful experience" are detrimental to the individual. In adapting to the modern world, meaningful experience requires the dissemination of knowledge. The culture of modern societies cannot depend upon an uninformed public opinion. Public *knowledge* has become a prerequisite for the well-being, if not the survival, of societies and of humanity.

Functionalism Analysis

Contributions to functionalism have been made by Emile Durkheim, Bronislaw Malinowski, Talcott Parsons, and others. However, I shall emphasize the views of Robert K. Merton. Not only have his writings been clear and influential but also their relationship to social problems is very pertinent.

Functional analysis, a term often used interchangeably with structural functionalism, is concerned with the interrelationship of social units. "*Functions* are those observed consequences which make for the adaptation or adjustment of a given system" (Merton, 1957:51). They refer to the ways in which the parts or units of a society work together. For example, a function of schools is to train members of society for employment in business and government.

Merton rejected certain views of his predecessors. He disagreed with the contention that every custom and practice was necessary, useful, or integrating for society. He contended that some established practices could be *dysfunctional,* that is, they might work against the adaptation of the whole.

These modifications are believed by Merton to have eliminated the conservative bias of structural functionalism. The critics have not been satisfied. They assert that "adaptation to the system" means maintaining its basic structures and goals (Gouldner, 1970:334; Friedrichs, 1971:26). It implies that outdated beliefs and practices are functional for traditional, static societies. Conversely, the introduction of new knowledge or modern techniques would be dysfunctional from this perspective.

Differences between manifest and latent functions have also been suggested by Merton. "*Manifest functions* are those objective consequences contributing to the adjustment or adaptation of the system which are intended and recognized by participants in the system; *latent functions,* correlatively, being those which are neither intended nor recognized" (1957:51).

Both function and dysfunction refer to the "objective" adaptive or maladaptive consequences of social phenomena. Whether a given social condition is adaptive or not is decided by functional analysis. The objective needs and requirements of the group are the criteria—not group members' beliefs nor their intentions.

The distinction between manifest and latent functions is based upon group intentions and awareness of such consequences. These "subjective" factors help to explain group behavior. However, judging the actual functions or dysfunctions of beliefs and practices is the job of the sociologist.

In studying social problems, Merton has taken an *apparently* similar, yet significantly different, viewpoint. Let us review his statement.

"Apart from manifest social problems—those objective social conditions identified by problem-definers as at odds with social values—are latent social problems, conditions that are also at odds with values current in the society but are not generally recognized as being so. The sociologist does not impose his values upon others when he undertakes to supply knowledge about latent social problems" (1971:806).

For functional analysis, the criteria of dysfunctions are the objectively maladaptive consequences of any social pattern. For social problems analysis, as defined by Merton, the criteria are subjective public values. Unless every popular preference is considered to be objectively adaptive, the two perspectives seem incompatible.

As functionalists, we may conclude that contemporary militarism, racism, or belief in occult healing is harmful to society. To the society that values any of these, however, the advocacy of peace, equality, or medical care would be a social problem. In such circumstances, adaptive, functional conditions are social problems, while dysfunctions are not.

Reconciling these paradigms has been attempted by Merton and by others. In doing so, Merton reveals the status quo tendency of functionalism. "The first point essential to using the concept of social dysfunction for the analysis of social problems is that ... social dysfunction refers to a *designated* set of consequences of a *designated* pattern of behavior, belief, or organization that interferes with a *designated* functional requirement of a *designated* social system" (1971:839). Presumably, the beliefs in freedom of speech by Solzhenitzyn were dysfunctional, as well as a social problem, for the Soviet Union.

A fundamental shortcoming of these views is their societal relativism. Established social structures and social values in a given society are the standards for identifying dysfunctions and social problems. In the absence of more universal criteria, such as the knowledge-values of science, the relativism of social stability or public preferences becomes the value standard of sociological analysis.

Power and Conflict

Dissatisfaction with prevailing paradigms has led some sociologists to propose alternative ones. Especially significant have been criticisms of the status quo assumptions about order and stability in societies. One of the most influential critics and innovators was C. Wright Mills. His ideas about power and conflict are having increasing impact upon sociology.

In one of his first books, with Hans Gerth, Mills traced the relationships between individual character and social structure (Gerth and Mills, 1953). Here, they drew together the ideas of Mead, Freud, Marx, and Weber. They asserted that personality and behavior could only be understood within the context of dominant social institutions and social processes.

Gerth and Mills described six "institutional orders" that have been "pivotal" in various societies. These are political, economic, military, religious, educational, and kinship. A master trend of the modern world is the growing dominance and unification of the political, economic, and military structures of society.

The latter trend in the United States was the focus of Mills' *The Power Elite*. He rejected the popular belief in an automatic social equilibrium of power, "with its assumptions of a plurality of independent, relatively equal, and conflicting groups of a balancing society" (1957:243). Government, big business, and the military establishment were described as collaborators in the control of American domestic and foreign policies.

A currently appropriate chapter concerned "the higher immorality" of the American power elite. Concentration of power in the hands of a few leads to disregard of the rights and aspirations of the many. Manipulation and deceit often seem necessary for those who control the mass society. I believe that the secrecy and deceptions over Vietnam and Watergate illustrate Mills' point.

In *The Causes of World War Three*, Mills examined the relationships between power and conflict and their consequences. To him, "all significant problems of man and society bear upon the issues of war and the politics of peace; and the solution to any significant problems in some part rests upon their outcome" (1958:22). His prediction may help to explain the failure of "the great society" to solve national problems while waging war.

Mills asserted that we live in constant danger of total annihilation. Powerful elites in Soviet Russia and the United States continually persuade their peoples of the need for improved weapons and larger military budgets. A misjudgment, a defective fail-safe mechanism, or a preemptive strike could trigger a global conflict.

Public knowledge and political action was urged to halt the arms race toward destruction. The role of science was considered important. Mills prodded scientists to develop a code of ethics and a public forum for their knowledge and for their unanswered questions.

A book of essays in honor of Mills bears the title *The New Sociology* (Horowitz, 1964). Its editor stated that "The new turn in sociology is thus an examination of large-scale problems" (1964:27). The contributors noted Mills' concern with the important and serious problems of our times. His criteria for identifying social problems were the values of freedom and reason (1959:130). Whatever imperiled those values was undesirable.

Critics and admirers have pointed out Mills' occasional oversimplifications and superficial research techniques (Rose, 1967; Goldsen, 1964). His efforts to develop a comparative, internationally oriented sociology were ended by his death at the age of forty-five in 1962. Still, his writings have helped to dispel popular myths, to avoid sociological triviality, and to focus inquiry upon significant problems.

The Sociology of Sociology

Sociologists have written many books and articles on such topics as race relations, marriage, education, social psychology, and social problems. There have been many also that describe the theories and research techniques of sociology. Until recently, there has been less concern with the discipline's premises, value assumptions, professional roles, and relationships to society.

Since the 1960s, a number of sociologists have begun to examine and write about the sociological enterprise. Reports on the patterns of recruitment, training, and employment of sociologists have appeared (Sibley, 1963), and professional concerns are the subject matter of *The American Sociologist,* which began publication in 1965.

The sociology of sociology has become a new field of study, making use of sociological concepts, theories, and research methods. It views sociology as a group activity, a part of society involving relationships to other groups, and is concerned with the beliefs, values, norms, roles, and self-conceptions of sociologists.

One of the recent studies is Robert Friedrichs' *A Sociology of Sociology* (1970), in which he applied Kuhn's ideas of "normal science" and "scientific paradigm" to sociology. The dominant paradigm in sociology during recent decades, according to Friedrichs, was functionalism. Under the "cloak of neutrality," the "normal sociology" was said to favor social system integration, stability, and conformity.

Friedrichs also used Kuhn's conception of "scientific revolutions," which are the new paradigms that emerge as a consequence of perceived anomalies in normal science. The sociological revolution involves more attention to social change and conflict, more concern with the values of sociology, and greater self-awareness. The sociology of sociology deals with such topics (see Reynolds and Reynolds, 1970).

In *The Coming Crisis of Western Sociology* (1970), Alvin W. Gouldner agrees that functionalism has been the dominant perspective of American sociology. He contends, like Friedrichs, that radical ideas, such as Marxism, have been avoided or oversimplified. To Gouldner, the crisis in sociology is the split between conservative, static theories and radical, change-oriented ones.

Much of his criticism was directed against the obscure writing and inconsistent viewpoints of Talcott Parsons. An eminent theorist, Parsons had proposed a "voluntaristic theory of action" in his early works (1937). Then, to Parsons, human behavior was not mechanical or automatic. Although social actions are influenced by past experience and existing conditions, he described them as active, creative and purposive.

Gouldner interpreted the later writings of Parsons as an essential reversal of the earlier position. In *The Social System* (1951), a functionalist analysis, Parsons presented the individual as a social product. "Man is a hollowed-out, empty being filled with substance only by society. Man thus is seen as an entirely *social* being, and the possibility of conflict between man and society is thereby reduced" (Gouldner, 1970:206).

Most important to Gouldner was Parsons' and other functionalists' allegedly conservative ideology. Such a viewpoint cannot adequately explain power, conflict, and change. Nor is it concerned with basic social problems; modifying dysfunctions sustains the system as it is.

Why call the approach "functionalism" rather than "dysfunctionalism," asks Gouldner? Functionalists are not value-free, as they claim. Conformity, adaptation, and system equilibrium are conservative concepts. However, we should note that some sociologists disagree with Gouldner's interpretations of Parsons' views and of functionalism (Turner, 1974).

Despite their past opposition, Gouldner sees a growing convergence between functionalism and Marxism. Soviet sociologists have been attracted to its status quo implications. Radical sociologists are remolding functionalism toward more change- and problem-oriented explanations. Gouldner believes that the crisis of divergent perspectives in sociology will have fruitful outcomes.

One of the products, to Gouldner, has been the new sociology of sociology. A "Reflexive Sociology"—sociology reflecting about itself—is Gouldner's recommendation. Such a sociology would not split the sociologist into a neutral scientist-technician on the one hand and an active citizen on the other.

To Gouldner, reflexive sociology is self-observing and

socially concerned. Sociologists who study themselves will recognize their similarities to other members of society and better understand their own roles, social relationships, and values. "A Reflexive Sociology would be a moral sociology" (1970:491).

I believe that such a sociology is emerging. Awareness of the implicit values of the so-called neutral sociology is increasing. Specifying the aims and responsibilities of sociology is a critical and needed effort. The outcome will have important consequences for the identification of social problems.

Toward Identifying Social Problems

Conceptions of social problems are linked intimately with the paradigms, theories, and methods of sociology. The preceding sections have dealt with some of the more notable ideas of influential sociologists. I have tried to summarize those views that apply to social problems analysis.

Drawing on these views, I aim to distinguish actual or real social problems from spurious or imaginary ones. I will also begin to consider ways to distinguish important or serious social problems from those that are trivial or minor. Chapter 4 will present my specific procedures for assessing seriousness.

The following section will examine the relevance of public conceptions of undesirable conditions for identifying social problems. Next will follow a discussion of appraisals by especially knowledgeable persons, which includes professional experts from psychiatry, law, social work, and so on. Thereafter, a discussion of sociological criteria will deal with differences between demonstrable and spurious social problems. Finally, the relationship between scientific knowledge-values and problem identification will be the final topic of the chapter.

The order in which these topics are presented is based

upon their *increasing* importance as criteria for identifying social problems. By applying these criteria, we can reduce or eliminate the anomalies resulting from other definitions of social problems.

Perceived Social Problems

One of the central shortcomings of the public opinion paradigm is the lack of specificity of its criteria of social problems. Most definitions refer to conditions considered to be undesirable by large or significant or influential numbers of people. We may rightfully ask, how large is large?

The present population of the United States is more than 200 million people. How many Americans must believe in the existence of an undesirable condition for it to be designated as a social problem?—100 million? 10 million? 250 thousand? Sociological definitions offer only vague guidance.

According to the definition, the beliefs and values of *small* numbers of people would not be appropriate for identifying a social problem. Minorities are excluded, thereby, from problem-defining. Instead, their divergent or new ideas and actions are the social problems.

Some sociologists have suggested that the number of concerned people is a measure of the magnitude of the social problem. In other words, the views of smaller numbers that some condition was harmful would represent only a minor or unimportant social problem. Numerical size determines what is good or bad.

Using the beliefs and values of large numbers of people is not suitable for identifying social problems in a changing, heterogeneous society. Attitudes toward the war in Vietnam illustrate the inadequacy. At the war's beginning, a small number of Americans were opposed to it. On the basis of numbers, the war was not a social problem. The vast majority of the people supported the war and viewed the critics as undesirable and unpatriotic. According to the definition, the critics were the social problem.

What is perceived as undesirable is important to sociology. Knowing what people believe to be harmful is needed in order to understand what they do. A much cited statement by one of the founders of the social disorganization paradigm makes a useful point. "If men define situations as real, they are real in their consequences" (Thomas, 1928:584).

The consequences of "definitions of the situation" can be real. However, one's definition may be erroneous. For example, a student may fail an exam because of the belief that studying for it is hopeless. The failure is a consequence of the defined situation. Whether the perception is correct or not is another question.

The accuracy of public perceptions and evaluations cannot be determined by sheer size alone. Large numbers of people, at times, are manipulated by modern techniques of mass persuasion. An apparent crime wave may be a reflection of sensational news reporting. Political candidates, doomsday evangelists, and advertising are frequent influences upon public opinion.

An example of influences upon public beliefs about undesirable conditions is the contemporary advertising campaign to arouse widespread concern over "body odors." Each year, deodorant manufacturers spend an estimated $40 million on advertisements (Consumers Union, 1974:160). Their efforts have led to consumer expenditures of more than $400 million yearly for mouth, underarm, genital, and foot deodorants. Apparently, millions of people have accepted the idea that body odors are undesirable conditions.

We do not know how many persons are aware of the possible hazards of deodorant usage. Some deodorants have been linked to skin irritations, illnesses, and deaths. Scientists have warned that propellants in deodorants and other spray products may endanger the protective ozone in the earth's atmosphere. Thus far, there does not appear to be any wide public fear of these consequences.

Identifying perceptions of undesirable conditions helps to explain what people will do. They are also helpful in focusing sociological attention upon actually harmful conditions. Public opinion is a necessary source of sociological knowledge. It must be recognized, however, as insufficient and perhaps misleading. We need to distinguish between popular perceptions and scientific knowledge.

Perceived social problems are those social conditions that are identified by groups or individuals as contrary to their group or personal values (Manis, 1974a:314). This definition does not rely upon size or numbers. Neither the beliefs of the few nor of the many are excluded. Whatever is considered undesirable by *any* members of society is a *perceived* social problem from that perspective.

The definition may be clarified by a comparison with the manifest-latent dichotomy proposed by Robert K. Merton. Although the terminology appears somewhat similar, there are important differences. To Merton, "The first and basic ingredient of a social problem consists of a substantial discrepancy between widely shared standards and actual conditions of social life" (1971:799). These "widely shared standards" must mean the values of many people.

Manifest social problems, as described by Merton, are the conditions contrary to widely held values *and* recognized by many people. Latent social problems are those conditions contrary to social values but which "are not generally recognized as being so" (1971:806).

First, perceived social problems are *not* restricted to conditions that are "generally recognized." We do not ignore the beliefs of minority groups or of individuals. Studying their perceptions is needed for understanding their behavior as well as the reactions of larger numbers. The manifest-latent categories deal solely with the latter.

Second, perceived social problems are not equated

with "real" ones. Whether they exist or not is a separate issue. The manifest-latent categories use social values as the standards for identifying social problems. For Merton, what many people deem undesirable *is* a social problem. As we have seen, using popular values as criteria is not neutral nor appropriate for the knowledge-values of science.

Adjudicated Social Problems

To many people throughout the world, a large family has been an established social value. Having many children has been a moral goal, esteemed for its own sake. Children have been prized also as proof of masculine virility and feminine fertility. In poorer countries, they are useful producers and future protectors of their aging parents.

These values have been opposed by family planners, psychiatrists, and other knowledgeable specialists. Demographers have been concerned over the rapid growth of world population, now doubling every thirty-five years. Agronomists have pointed out that more than 90 percent of the world's arable land is already in use. Some experts predicted, during the 1960s, that massive starvation would occur in underdeveloped countries by the mid-1970s (Paddock and Paddock, 1967).

According to popular values, at least in the recent past, large families and rapid population growth were not social problems. Nor were environmental pollutants identified as undesirable by the public. Heroin addiction also was not considered to be a social problem until it began to affect the white majority. Its prevalence in the nonwhite slums had been recognized by police, physicians, and social workers for several decades prior to the public's concern.

The public opinion paradigm subordinates objective conditions to subjective interpretations. That is, a condition cannot be a social problem unless many people think it is undesirable. In a sense, we are reversing the relationships. Widespread beliefs and values may lead us toward an awareness of objectively harmful conditions. Our aim is to arrive at more objective criteria.

The knowledge and values of technical specialists, experts, and other well-informed observers offer a step in the right direction. *Adjudicated social problems* are those conditions in society deemed harmful by knowledgeable people. Among them we may include legal specialists, urban planners, medical personnel, and engineers.

These sources are relevant within their own areas of technical competence (and as we shall see, not always there). Official information about crime, medical knowledge about fluoridation, and social worker experience with family problems can be compared with the beliefs and values held by the public. Comparisons need not imply superiority or assured accuracy. They facilitate the investigation of social problems.

Knowledgeable people are not limited to the professions. As Blumer has suggested to researchers, "One should sedulously seek participants in the sphere of life who are acute observers and who are well informed. One such person is worth a hundred others who are merely unobservant participants" (1969:41). Not large numbers of people alone but "acute observers" are needed to identify real social problems.

What is considered harmful by "experts" is not always in accord with public awareness or social values. Their views need to be considered by sociologists. *Unrecognized social problems* are those conditions deemed harmful by knowledgeable persons that are not so identified by other members of society.

Taking another example, many physicians, legal authorities, and recovered alcoholics have been aroused over the rising rates of alcoholism. Until recently, many people seemed unaware or unconcerned. In their case, alcoholism has been an unrecognized social problem. We expect that among the various groups in society there will be differences in awareness or lack of awareness of harmful conditions.

Designating and locating knowledgeable people is no easy task. Still, despite their reliance upon public opinion for identifying social problems, sociologists usually defer to experts in their analysis of these problems. Delinquency is said to be a social problem because many people believe it is undesirable. Still, legal criteria are used by sociologists in deciding who and what is delinquent.

All of us are aware that experts do not agree on every important issue. Experts also change their minds. Only recently has the American Psychiatric Association decided that homosexuality is not a form of mental disorder. Their action was far from unanimous.

In these circumstances, the task of the sociologist is especially difficult. Resolving disagreements between experts, as between experts and the public, requires careful sociological judgment. Before making such judgments, we need to specify our own criteria for determining what is and what is not a social problem.

Demonstrable Social Problems

Public interpretations of undesirable conditions have been accepted, with sporadic questioning by sociologists, in identifying social problems. In some ways sociologists have been more critical of the views of experts. As illustrations, I shall take up the controversies over homosexuality and mental illness.

Homosexuality is considered undesirable behavior by many people (Simmons, 1969:33). In most states, homosexual acts are violations of criminal law, punishable by lengthy prison sentences. Until 1974, the confirmed homosexual was diagnosed as mentally ill by psychiatry. Textbooks continue to describe homosexuality as a social problem.

Certain sociologists have expressed their reservations about these viewpoints. To them, homosexual behavior is victimless crime (Schur, 1965). Homosexual relationships between consenting adults need not be injurious to the individuals nor to society. Those who urge decriminalization and social tolerance of homosexuality stress its lack of harm or damage to people.

Similar arguments may be raised about other forms of disapproved behavior. The "generation gap" is used to explain many unconventional life-styles—in dress, long hair, communes, meditation, pacificism, and marihuana. Their harmfulness is open to question.

A medical summary contends that "there are no lasting ill effects from the acute use of marihuana and no fatalities have ever been reported" (Jaffee, 1969:49). According to the same source, "there seems to be growing agreement within the medical community, at least, that marijuana does not directly cause criminal behavior, juvenile delinquency, sexual excitement, or addiction" (1969:51).

These remarks are not intended to approve or justify violation of social norms or laws. They are used to illustrate that what is perceived as a social problem need not have the assumed harmful consequences. *Demonstrable social problems* are social conditions identified as detrimental to human well-being on the basis of reasonable evidence. *Hypothetical social problems* are social conditions assumed to be harmful on the basis of reasonable interpretations or theories.

I have suggested the latter conception because there are many deficiencies in our knowledge about individuals and society. For instance, there is substantial controversy over the concept of mental illness. Various forms of human behavior are diagnosed as mental illness by psychiatrists. Critics have doubted the relevance of "illness" as an explanation of disapproved behavior. One eminent psychiatrist has written about "the myth of mental illness" (Szasz, 1961).

Opponents do not deny the existence of such organic conditions as paresis and senility. Their objections are to the labeling and institutionalization of people who appear to be a burden, such as the aged, or nonconforming, such as the young (Scheff, 1966). We need to decide whether it is these people or their "treatment" that are objectively harmful conditions.

It is clear that some perceived social problems are the results of popular misconceptions and biases. Public fears of witches, long hair, fluoridation, and homosexuality are not grounded on factual knowledge. *Spurious social problems* are those perceived social problems that are not contrary to personal or group values or are not detrimental to human well-being.

The criteria for identifying demonstrable or spurious social problems differ from those used in identifying perceived social problems. The latter require information about the beliefs, values, and communications of the appropriate group membership. Several sociologists have called people's efforts to understand troublesome conditions "quasi-theories." "It is in the social context of talk that problematic conditions become defined. Everyday talk about problems is clearly not conducted according to the rigorous criteria of scientific rationality" (Hewitt and Hall, 1973:369). They suggest that sociologists study such quasi-theories in order to explain how people come to define what is problematic.

Scientific theories and empirical data are criteria used by sociologists to distinguish between demonstrable and spurious social problems. Such theories and data are more "rigorous criteria" than "everyday talk." Applying these criteria can help to determine which of the quasi-theories or perceived social problems are demonstrable and which are spurious.

We can admit that sociological criteria are not as rigorous as we would wish them to be. They are available, and they are improving. Sociologists are amassing an expanded body of factual knowledge. Research techniques are increasingly sophisticated. We need not be restricted to studying the conceptions of undesirable conditions held by large or significant numbers of people.

Deciding which social phenomena are likely to be injurious and which are not is a central task of social problems analysis. In some cases, the identification of social problems will need to be provisional. Whether violence on public television and in the movies is a beneficial catharsis or a dangerous stimulus is uncertain. Nor can we be certain about the potential consequences of widespread marihuana usage.

The identification of a social problem does not depend solely upon factual or theoretical knowledge. Value standards will be the final, determining criteria. I have proposed that the knowledge-values of science be used as the basis of sociological judgments of social problems. We need to examine their relevance for problem identification.

Knowledge-Values and Social Problems

"Our problems are all in areas that are deeply involved with certain ethical judgments, while our social scientists, committed to an ideal of objective neutrality, are most reluctant to venture into the realm of ethics" (Means, 1969:1). Natural scientists have also been reluctant to do so. Still, the influence of values cannot be excluded from the search for knowledge.

We have seen that government funding policies increasingly channel scientific inquiry. Likewise, the employment of scientists in commerce and industry affects their activities. The goals of national power and corporate gain, however, are not congruent with the so-called ethical neutrality nor the proposed knowledge-values of science.

To say that science is guided by values is not to deny its attempts at accuracy, precision, and objectivity. These are appropriate values. So, too, are the values of freedom to question established viewpoints, of communicating research findings, and, I would add, of responsibility to humanity.

As a physicist-philosopher has commented, "Man is an animal, and animals cannot live and survive nonevaluatively" (Miller, 1973:1). She noted also that human beings are more conscious, rational, and knowledgeable in their evaluations. In my view, these characteristics are especially applicable to the scientific enterprise. The knowledge-values of science can help to resolve some of the unanswered questions of problem identification.

Let us take some concrete examples. The intrinsic values of science will be our starting point. I have suggested that empirical knowledge—knowledge based on evidence—is one of the intrinsic values. I have used this value in referring to demonstrable social problems. The latter, rather than widespread belief, is appropriate for sociological judgments of supposedly harmful conditions.

A case in point involves popular conceptions of racial differences. Many apparent differences in racial abilities, motivation, aggression, and criminality have been linked to social conditioning. Yet, some people consider these differences to be entirely hereditary. Such unsupported ideas may lead them to view efforts aimed at equality or integration as undesirable and hopeless. In their view, the efforts are the social problems.

Scientists value empirical knowledge. Based on this value, sociologists are expected to avoid judgments derived from personal prejudices or established traditions. I have called judgments of undesirability based upon erroneous ideas spurious social problems.

As sociologists, we need to investigate perceived social problems. Spurious or not, public perceptions need study in order to interpret and predict group behavior. However, we must distinguish facts from fictions. We must also advance our understanding of what is beneficial and what is injurious to people. The contemporary study of values can aid our efforts. Applying the knowledge-values of science is a step in this direction.

For many perceived social problems we do not have adequate information. In such cases, we must admit that our interpretations are hypothetical. Hypotheses and empirical data are related to another intrinsic value of science, theoretical knowledge. Theories guide our search for understanding. They tell us what is worth seeking.

Good theories help to explain the world around us. As Robert S. Lynd has commented, "There is 'idle' curiosity and 'focused' curiosity, but in the world of science there is no such thing as 'pure' curiosity" (1939:182–183). He pointed out that scientists do not bother counting all the grains of sand on miles of seashore; economists don't check the dates on coins received at stores; sociologists don't compare the bricks in slum buildings. There is much we could study; theories guide us toward important knowledge.

The intrinsic value of theoretical knowledge is a helpful criterion for identifying social problems. Theory can help to distinguish what is actually detrimental to human beings from what is not. For example, labeling theory has questioned traditional beliefs through the concept of victimless crimes, such as homosexuality. Theory can also help us to distinguish important social problems from minor or trivial ones. The latter topic will be discussed in Chapter 4.

The contextual values of science are another source of criteria for identifying social problems. One of these values is freedom of inquiry. Barriers to free inquiry prevent advances in our knowledge.

Federal restrictions upon scientific research are illustrative. Studies of the effects of marihuana declined sharply over a period of several decades. The decline has been attributed to difficulties in obtaining legal permission to study marihuana and to obtain it for research (Lingeman, 1969:143). As a consequence, the perceived problem of marihuana usage led to the demonstrable problem of societal ignorance of its actual effects.

A related problem is the control and concealment of scientific knowledge. Many of us have heard of such influences in Soviet Russia. We may be less aware of such secrecy in American governmental and business policies. An example is concealment of the dangerous side effects of certain pharmaceuticals. Another is the long-hidden study of how we became involved in Vietnam—later revealed by the Ellsberg case.

Interference with the release of research findings is contrary to the contextual value of freedom of expression. Scientists need to have access to the data and conclusions of their colleagues. Barriers to scientific communication and lack of support of inquiry make it difficult to identify and appraise social problems.

The social responsibility values of science are relevant to the suppression of data or theories by their opponents. On occasion, community residents have sought to ban discussion of the theory of evolution in their schools. The implications of the theory have appeared undesirable, harmful, or irreligious to them—a perceived social problem. From the perspective of the communality values, the ban on the theory is the harmful condition.

Scientific knowledge is not advanced solely by Ph.D.-holders. Students, journalists, missionaries, housewives, and other knowledge-seekers have contributed to the sciences, from anthropology to zoology. Sharing public knowledge is part of the knowledge-values of science. Restrictions on knowledge are social problems.

The social responsibility value of meliorism is directly pertinent to the identification of social problems. As I have described it, meliorism is the obligation of science to avoid harm and to "do good" for humanity. This does not mean that sociologists should be engaged only in practical research. It does mean more awareness of scientific purposes and their potential consequences.

Scientists cannot expect to predict or control all the outcomes of their data. Few discoveries and innovations have purely beneficial or detrimental results. Research findings about social learning may be applicable for education and for propaganda. Knowledge of viruses can be used for healing and for warfare.

Unless there are compelling reasons to the contrary, we should not impede the search for knowledge. Rather, it would be wiser to accelerate research aimed at identifying and analyzing socially harmful conditions.

The most debatable of the social responsibility values is that of activism. Most scientists and their professional associations have been reluctant, or even strongly opposed, to recommend social policies. However, the dangers of nuclear radiation, pesticides, food additives, population growth, and war have aroused many others. Their identification of socially harmful conditions has led them to advocate societal awareness and action.

There remain unanswered major issues involving the social responsibility values. Should we permit the test of a hypothesis concerning a potentially unending nuclear explosion that blows up everything? Should information about nuclear fission become public knowledge? Should molecular biologists experiment with genetic changes detrimental to human survival? Should human beings be guinea pigs in risky chemical, psychological, or social experiments?

The preceding ethical questions are not merely hypothetical. Decisions concerning these and similar issues are being made more often by powerful elites than by an informed public. The consequences will be crucial for humanity.

All of us need to be aware of the real, important conditions that affect our lives. The suggested knowledge-values of science can be of help in understanding our problems. My presentation of these criteria is one attempt to deal with them. They are provisional efforts open to discussion, questioning, and change. I believe such discussion is needed in order to distinguish our real problems from our imaginary ones.

Summary

In this chapter I have discussed the relationships of major theoretical paradigms to the study of social problems. Despite substantial differences between symbolic interactionism and functionalism, leading exponents of these perspectives consider social problems as the subjective concerns of group members. Their critics have stressed the need to deal with such objective social forces as power and conflict. The sociology of sociology has encouraged reexamination of the basic assumptions and values of the field.

Using the subjective approach, we can locate perceived social problems—those social conditions that are identified by groups or individuals as contrary to their group or personal values. Adjudicated social problems are conditions deemed harmful by knowledgeable people, such as professional experts, while unrecognized social problems are the harmful conditions that are not identified by other members of society.

We need to carefully appraise popular and expert judgments of social conditions. For the sociologist, demonstrable social problems are conditions deemed detrimental to human well-being on the basis of reasonable evidence; hypothetical social problems are the conditions assumed to be harmful on the basis of reasonable interpretations and theories; spurious social problems are the perceived social problems that are not contrary to group values or are not detrimental to human well-being. Scientific knowledge-values offer criteria for making these appraisals.

In Chapter 4, I intend to examine procedures for assessing the seriousness of social problems. Three measures of seriousness—magnitude, severity, and primacy—will be explained. The topics of data collection and analysis will precede descriptions of the major types of data used in the study of social problems.

RECOMMENDED READING

Blumer, Herbert. "Social Problems as Collective Behavior." *Social Problems* 18 (Winter 1971):298. A symbolic interactionist justification for using public conceptions as criteria of social problems.

———. *Symbolic Interactionism: Perspective and Method.* Englewood Cliffs, N.J.: Prentice-Hall, 1969. The first chapter contains a clear statement of symbolic interactionism by its leading contemporary spokesman.

Friedrichs, Robert W. *A Sociology of Sociology.* New York: Free Press, 1970. Drawing on Kuhn's conception of scientific paradigms, the author critically appraises the basic assumptions and polarizations of sociology.

Gouldner, Alvin W. *The Coming Crisis of Western Sociology.* New York: Basic Books, 1970. The crisis of sociology, according to the author, grows out of its dependence on the static ideas of functionalism. Reflexive Sociology is the topic of the provocative final chapter.

Hewitt, John P., and Peter M. Hall, "Social Problems, Problematic Situations, and Quasi-Theories." *American Sociological Review* 38 (June 1973):367–374. In this article the authors view popular interpretations of social problems as "quasi-theories." The interpretation parallels those suggested in preceding sections.

Manis, Jerome G. "Common Sense Sociology and Analytic Sociology." *Sociological Focus* 5 (Spring 1972):1–15. This article deals with the frequent mixing of public beliefs and objective data in such sociological concepts as functionalism, social class, and social roles.

Means, Richard L. *The Ethical Imperative: The Crisis in American Values.* Garden City, N.Y.: Doubleday, 1969. The author points out the limitations of ethical neutrality for dealing with the critical breakdown of values in American society.

Merton, Robert K. *On Theoretical Sociology.* New York: Free Press, 1967. A paperback edition containing important essays by a leading contributor to functionalism. Chapter III includes a discussion of manifest and latent functions.

Mills, C. Wright. *The Power Elite.* New York: Oxford University Press, 1957. Despite criticisms of its data and interpretations, this classic study remains an important contribution to a difficult and critical topic.

———. *The Causes of World War Three.* New York: Ballantine Books, 1958. Written for the general public, the book deals with a problem often avoided by other sociologists.

Rose, Arnold. *The Power Structure.* New York: Oxford University Press, 1967. The author is critical of the Mills' contention that American society is controlled by a centralized power elite.

Schur, Edwin M. *Crimes Without Victims.* Englewood Cliffs, N.J.: Prentice-Hall, 1965. Using the deviance perspective, the book shows how certain laws result in the "criminalization" of offenders.

Smigel, Erwin O., ed. *Handbook on the Study of Social Problems.* Chicago: Rand McNally, 1971. A collection of informative articles reviews some of the major perspectives, research methods, and "representative" social problems.

Szasz, Thomas S. *The Myth of Mental Illness.* New York: Paul B. Hoeber, 1961. A practicing psychiatrist, in the first of many polemical books, takes issue with the central ideas of his profession.

4
Assessing Seriousness

". . . Millions of persons in the Near and Middle East suffer from poverty on the basis of any objective measure; however, as long as these millions do not consider their situation unjust or alterable, their poverty does not constitute a sizable social problem" (Tallman and McGee, 1971:42). Why not? In this view, the poverty of millions of people is not a sizable social problem because it is not believed to be so.

Definitions have consequences. What logical conclusion do we reach from the public opinion definition of social problems? The criterion is what people feel and believe, not the objective condition. The preceding quotation is based upon this premise. Hence, the size or magnitude of a social problem is decided by the extent of subjective concerns.

In this chapter, I shall compare subjective and objective standards for assessing the seriousness of social problems. Drawing upon the knowledge values of science, I shall discuss ways to distinguish between minor or trivial social problems and important or serious ones. My criterion will be the actual or potential harmfulness of social conditions.

As I have said, the use of scientific standards for judging

the importance of social problems does not imply a know-it-all science. Nor does it require the crowning of scientists. Rather, the aim is to improve our understanding both of perceptions and of reality. In order to do so, three criteria for appraising the seriousness of social problems will be presented. These are the primacy, the magnitude, and the severity of social problems. Separate sections will deal with each topic.

Determining seriousness requires the collection and analysis of adequate data. Appropriate research methods will be reviewed in the succeeding sections. Social records, such as official reports and statistics, are common sources of sociological information about social problems. Their usefulness and their shortcomings require our attention.

Direct observation of social problems would be most desirable. Unfortunately, there are many difficulties that have limited efforts to apply this method. Instead, sociologists have tended to rely upon opinion survey techniques. Both procedures merit discussion.

Cross-national studies are the subject matter of comparative sociology. Although comparative researches have long been advocated by sociologists, relatively few have been conducted in the past. They are, however, on the increase. Judgment of the seriousness of social problems would be facilitated by such methods.

Evaluation research is a recent development in sociology. This type of research was developed to study the effectiveness of social action programs. Their attempts at cost-benefit calculations have important implications for assessing the seriousness of social problems as well as the efforts aimed at their solution.

Some of the research methods, such as surveys, are well established. Others, like evaluation techniques, are in their infancy. I shall investigate their usefulness for appraising seriousness while trying to avoid exaggerated claims of relevance or of accuracy.

Perceived and Demonstrable Seriousness

In modern societies, public evaluations of undesirable conditions often parallel those by scientists. Many persons are well-informed; others are less knowledgeable. In less modern societies, the majority is apt to be dominated by traditional, outdated beliefs. Using the amount of popular concern as the standard of seriousness is equally outdated.

A historical example of imagined perils is the seventeenth-century belief in heresy and witchcraft. "During the first six decades of settlement in Massachusetts, three serious 'crime waves' occurred which affected the young colony in decisive ways. Each of these waves became an object of wide public concern" (Erikson, 1966:67). The alleged crimes included "activities of the Devil." The evidence was often only rumor or hearsay. The punishments were jail, whipping, torture, banishment, or death.

Though a few prominent individuals were critical, there was "wide public concern" over these supposedly serious crimes. Our advantage of hindsight suggests that the fears were senseless and destructive. Yet, the public opinion paradigm accepts the widespread belief as evidence of a serious social problem.

A modern equivalent of the witch-hunt took place during the 1950s. Many people believed that the Department of State was infested with homosexuals, subversives, and communist sympathizers. A 1950 Gallup poll found that only 20 percent of those interviewed doubted the charges of communist infiltration; more than twice as many approved or believed (Gallup, 1972:I, 924). A United States senator aroused and led the public outcry against alleged traitors. Not long afterward, however, McCarthyism came to mean malicious or unjustified charges of wrongdoing.

These are illustrations of erroneous or exaggerated ideas. They involve spurious or minor social problems. We require more verifiable evidence than the beliefs of large numbers of people. The *perceived seriousness* of social problems will refer to the interpretations by group members about the degree of harmfulness of social conditions. Such perceptions deserve to be investigated but should not limit our inquiry.

Commonsense descriptions of undesirable conditions are useful sociological data. In various ways, each person engages in practical everyday sociology, psychology, economics, and so on. Understanding of people, prices, and politics are necessary in the everyday experience of social relationships, buying groceries, and supporting candidates for public office. Evaluating the damage produced by social conflict, inflation, or corruption can be facilitated by studying the conventional wisdom.

Personal experience is instructive to the individual. The burnt child, we say, avoids the fire. Pain, illness, threats, and degradation are subjective consequences of objective realities. Neither a college degree nor a research project is needed to reveal the undesirability of disease or oppression. Studying subjective interpretations helps to account for behavior and to locate truly harmful situations.

The individual's commonsense thinking about everyday life is affected by direct experience and by information from others. Education, tradition, propaganda, and rumor also are influential. The sources of social perceptions are an often unclear and unquestioned mixture. Sorting out the misjudgments from the accurate appraisals of the socially detrimental is necessary.

By *demonstrable seriousness* is meant the degree to which objectively determined conditions are detrimental to human well-being. The impact of theoretical conditions for which there is insufficient evidence will be considered as *hypothetical seriousness*. For many social problems, we lack adequate data or are faced with contradictory findings. Such circumstances call for cautious appraisals.

We need also to consider carefully the differential impact of harmful conditions. Some people may be more greatly affected by these conditions than others. For example, the consequences of a recession tend to be more critical for young persons, racial minorities, and women. We must, therefore, specify for whom such conditions are important.

We shall look at three aspects or indicators of seriousness in the following sections: the magnitude, the severity, and the primacy of social problems. Although most sociologists define social problems as subjective conceptions, they usually rely upon such objective dimensions of seriousness in their analyses of the conditions.

Ideally, we should like to have precise measurements of each indicator. As we shall see, this is not possible. Nor shall we be able to combine them into a single comprehensive measure of total seriousness. Specifying our criteria and, later, our research techniques can lead us toward improved understanding of critical social problems.

Magnitude

The simplest, most measurable, and best documented indicator of the seriousness of social problems is their *magnitude.* The term will be used to describe the size or the extent of a social problem. Elsewhere, magnitude has referred to the amount of public concern—the number of concerned persons and the degree of their discontent (Tallman and McGee, 1971:42).

The magnitude of public concern differs from the *perceived magnitude of social problems.* The latter pertains to the beliefs that people have about the extent of undesirable conditions. Obviously, the belief that there is much drug abuse may raise the general level of opposition. However, belief and reality are not always identical.

The knowledge-values of science suggest that these perceptions be subjected to empirical investigation. An intrinsic value of science is accurate, verifiable knowledge. Challenging unsupported beliefs about magnitude is a social responsibility of science.

What appears to be a "crime wave" may be a product of increased criminality, improved police records, or sensational news media. (An interesting description of the latter is the chapter "I Make a Crime Wave" in Steffens (1931:285–291). On the other hand, concealment or failure to report crimes results in underestimating the actual magnitude of crimes. A later section will inspect the accuracy of official reports of social problems.

The total numbers of persons affected by crime, mental disorder, or poverty are indicators of the magnitude of social problems. Their magnitude can be specified in the form of percentages or rates for the entire society or for subgroups. While the total amount of adult crimes exceeds those committed by juveniles, there are far fewer juveniles. As a consequence, the ratio of juvenile offenders to the youthful population is greater than it is for adults. This is due, also, to the greater number of laws applicable only to children and young people.

Although most sociologists rely on public opinion in deciding what is or is not a social problem, few are concerned with public beliefs about their magnitude. Instead, they draw upon the best available sources of information—reported frequencies, prevalence, or rates. Whatever their shortcomings, such data are preferable to unsupported assumptions, however widely accepted the latter may be.

Aside from deficiencies in reported data, there are difficulties in comparisons of the magnitude of different social problems. "Shall we conclude that the approximately 9000 murders in 1969 represent about one-fifth as great a social problem as the approximately 56,700 deaths from vehicular accidents in that year?" (Merton, 1971:801). Although the questioner responded negatively, we may ask, why not? We can agree that their causes were different, and that public apathy toward traffic fatalities differs from public concern over homicide.

The most important feature of these conditions is their

outcome—socially generated deaths. Like war-related fatalities, they are produced by human beings. Their magnitude can be compared by enumerating their occurrence. Vital statistics lead us to the *demonstrable magnitude* of social problems.

The magnitude of many other social problems is less accessible to measurement. Disputes over the numbers of child abuse cases, alcoholics, and drug addicts remain unsolved. Certainly, more research is needed—a standard sociological assertion. Estimates of magnitude by knowledgeable people, however, are preferable to those held by a less well-informed populace.

Questionable estimates of magnitude make for questionable comparisons. Are the estimated 9 million alcoholics a greater social problem than the estimated 600,000 drug addicts (Horton and Leslie, 1974:539, 552)? Despite the probable error in these estimates, we can hypothesize that alcoholism is far greater in magnitude than other drug addictions.

Magnitude is only one indicator of the seriousness of social problems. Their actual harmfulness to individuals and to society are highly important. To the public, alcoholism is less fearful than heroin addiction. A federal report, however, has asserted that "alcohol abuse accounts for far more destruction than any known psychoactive substance" (cited in Stewart, 1972:339). Their comparisons of destructiveness involve magnitude *and* consequences of the problems.

Most arguable are comparisons of very different social problems. "Assessing the magnitude of poverty requires different standards from those used in appraising the rates of juvenile delinquency. Are equal numbers of the poor and of juvenile delinquents equivalent in seriousness as social problems? Though their differences appear to defy attempts to compare their magnitude, the effort to do so is important" (Manis, 1974b:12). Making judgments cannot be excluded from the study of social problems.

Comparing the magnitude of social problems calls for knowledge of their specific effects. The severity of the effects of alcohol or heroin addiction is a related indicator of their seriousness. I shall take up that indicator in the next section.

Severity

The contextual values of science are applicable to the study of severity. Among these values, I have included freedom of inquiry, human well-being, and preservation of the human environment. Viewing science as public knowledge suggests such criteria are relevant for appraising social problems.

By *severity*, I mean the actual harmfulness of social problems for individuals, societies, and humanity. A nuclear war would be more destructive than a conventional war. Loss of life is clearly a more harmful outcome of war than minor wounds.

What is perceived as severity is often subject to controversy. Disagreements still flourish over the presumed social or personal damage of homosexual acts and the use of marihuana. Despite the uncertainties, both are opposed by law and custom. Smoking cigarettes is legal and popular, although, officially and empirically, it is "dangerous to your health."

We can begin our discussion of severity with demonstrably harmful conditions, those affecting the physical well-being of the individual. The degree of severity ranges from the finality of death through major and minor physical incapacity. These categories are crude but useful ways of assessing harmful conditions. For example, deaths, whether stemming from automobile accidents, quarrels, or warfare, are equivalent in severity. Less severe are disabling injuries, whatever their causes may be.

Temporarily harmful conditions are less severe than

enduring, recurring, or permanent ones. Addictive drugs are properly considered to be more harmful than non-addictive drugs. The medical concern with chronic illness and the penologist's concern with recidivism reflect this aspect of severity.

Similar judgments have been made concerning mental disorders. A diagnostic manual of the American Psychiatric Association (1968) has considered psychiatric impairment in terms of mild to severe categories. Their diagnoses are based on the ability of the individual to perform necessary social and occupational duties.

Criminal laws are expected to assign penalties on the basis of assumed social injury. A twenty-year prison sentence is a more severe penalty than a one-year term; these differences in penalties are imposed in accordance with some judgment of differing criminal severity.

The Federal Bureau of Investigation categorizes crimes on the basis of their alleged seriousness (*Uniform Crime Reports,* 1973:vi). The bureau's Crime Index Offenses include homicide and aggravated assault, while disorderly conduct is excluded. Some sociologists have proposed the decriminalization of acts that are not harmful to the individual or society. Crimes without victims refer, in the judgment of many criminologists, to misconceived ideas of social injury.

Popular or traditional perceptions of severity need to be identified. Knowledge of these perceptions is helpful in explaining public reactions to social problems. They also need to be compared with the actual degree of severity. To say this is not to imply that appraisals of severity are readily decided. Recognizing *demonstrable severity* is an important aspect of social problems analysis.

Comparisons of the magnitude of social problems require appraisals of their severity. As I have mentioned earlier, traffic fatalities are comparable to homicides in terms of their severe outcomes. The severity of such other problems as poverty, of course, is more difficult to judge.

No implication is intended that such judgments can be made easily.

Using magnitude as an indicator of the importance of social problems assumes that their extent implies severity. Higher levels of mental disorder, alcoholism, and traffic fatalities are more injurious to society than lesser amounts. Some may assume that white-collar crime is less critical than other types of crime, while others contend just the opposite.

A former program officer of the Federal Trade Commission contended that "the total value of property taken from individuals by robbery in the United States in 1968 is estimated at less than $55 million, whereas detectable business frauds netted in excess of one *billion* dollars in the same year" (Cox, Fellmeth, Schulz, 1969:194). If this is correct, business fraud is the more sizable problem.

Estimates of the severity of social problems call for information about their social benefits. What is damaging to one group may be helpful to others. Thus, poverty offers many advantages to the non-poor. A sociologist has enumerated fifteen of the "positive functions" of poverty in the United States (Gans, 1972). These included the performance of "dirty work," consumption of used products, and maintaining employment for police, social workers, and pawnshops.

Calculating the precise costs and benefits of social problems is not possible. Data concerning magnitude and severity remain sparse or contradictory. Much of our analyses will have to be hypothetical rather than demonstrable. Reasoned evaluations using available evidence remain preferable to the often questionable beliefs of large numbers of people.

Primacy

The study of serious social problems can be aided by comparisons of their harmful consequences. Social problems that have many severe effects are more serious than those with lesser ones. Stated simply, by the *primacy* of social problems is meant their causal importance as harmful conditions.

To illustrate, let us first take up the injurious consequences of automobile usage. These include pollution, energy shortages, traffic fatalities, and many more. On the other hand, there are numerous advantages—employment, profits, transportation, recreation, and so on. Reduction of vehicle usage could be beneficial, but complete elimination would be impractical and costly.

By comparison, the net effects of a nuclear war would be wholly detrimental for humanity. Massive destruction of life, health, property, and environment are among the predictable outcomes. The possible benefits are insignificant. The inevitable losses from such a conflict unquestionably are greater than those of traffic problems, alcoholism, or homosexuality.

Primary social problems are those social conditions that have many harmful consequences. For example, we may hypothesize that poverty tends to produce or facilitate malnutrition, shorter life expectancy, desertion, and drug addiction. If the effects of each of the latter problems are less detrimental, then poverty should be of greater concern to us. For simplification, the functions or benefits of social problems will not be considered at this point.

The primacy of social problems should be distinguished from their magnitude and their severity. For example, the magnitude of drug addiction means the size of the problem, that is, the number of addicts and the extent of drug usage. The severity of drug abuse refers to the degree of its specific harmfulness, for example, health or work performance. Appraising its primacy requires information about magnitude and severity. However, primacy will apply specifically to the totality of its causal influences, direct and indirect.

Drug addiction is known to be most prevalent among the poor and the blacks of American society. On these grounds, we hypothesize that poverty and racism are the more important underlying causes or antecedents of addiction. Poverty and racism are more likely to be primary social problems; their many consequences can be designated as secondary or tertiary problems.

By *secondary social problems* is meant those harmful conditions resulting from primary social problems that, in turn, lead to additional problems. *Tertiary social problems* are the consequences, direct or indirect, of more influential social problems. A diagram of the hypothetical relationships between these categories of social problems is presented in Figure 1.

It has been asserted that "the theme of white supremacy has always been an integral and pervasive feature of the American system" (Killian, 1968:16). If this assertion is true, racism is not an American social problem according to the public opinion paradigm. I would argue, to the contrary, that racism is a primary social problem.

Upon this assumption, segregation and discrimination are secondary social problems, that is, products of racism. The harmful effects of segregation and discrimination can be viewed as tertiary social problems. Among them are unemployment, alienation, and, possibly, violent crime.

The three levels of primacy are proposed in order to aid in the assessment of seriousness. Social problems that produce many more harmful conditions are more critical to society than those with lesser results. Of course, unraveling the chain of cause-effect relationships is difficult. Societies are complex and changing. Recognition of the difficulties, however, must not halt our inquiries. It may be that our notable failure to solve many social problems is due to our lack of knowledge of their interrelationships. The suggested distinctions offer guidelines for problem-solving.

Figure 1. A Diagram for Classifying Social Problems on the Basis of Hypothesized Influences*

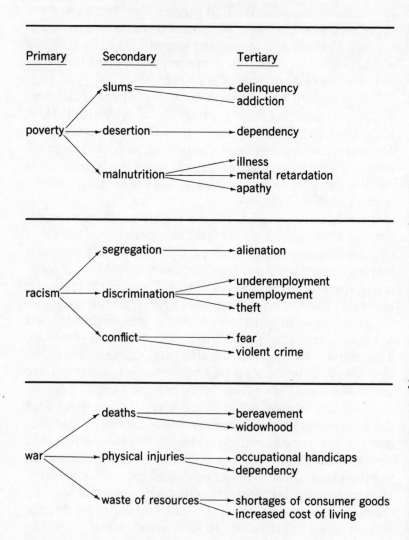

*Manis 1974b:10.

The term primary social problems is not intended to imply the existence of uncaused conditions. It is used only to emphasize the greater importance of certain problems at a given point in time. The specific examples represent hypothesized, rather than demonstrable, influences. Our knowledge of the interrelationships between social problems remains limited.

These comments are applicable to the illustrations of secondary and tertiary social problems. Distinctions between them, as with other social phenomena, will require further inquiry. We must also note that tertiary social problems have detrimental effects. By definition, a social problem is a harmful condition. In referring to tertiary social problems, we merely stress their lower level of harmfulness.

Primary social problems often are established patterns of social relationships. Social institutions support and maintain them. Beliefs about racial and masculine superiority have been diffused by schools and taught in the home. They have been incorporated in law and enforced by police and courts.

Poverty is part of the system of social stratification. The structure of society determines the distribution of social benefits. How the economy and the political institutions operate affects the fate of the worker, the aged, young people, and minorities.

Clearly, appraising the level of primacy is no easy task. Yet, whether traceable to established or emerging social forces, the sources of harmful conditions must be identified if they are to be improved. We must not avoid the task because of its intricacy or its implications.

Careful, thorough study is needed in order to offset difficulties in determining the primacy, as well as the other seriousness indicators, of social problems. Hasty judgments and popular beliefs are no substitute for sociological analysis. The latter requires accurate, appropriate information and interpretations.

From Concepts to Data Collection

To study social problems, we need to know what to look for and how to find out about them. Consider the following statement: "No mode of human behavior can be considered a social problem, no matter how repugnant it may be to any given individual or small group, unless it is regarded as a morally objectionable deviance from some accepted norm, or norms, by a substantial and determining number of persons in the surrounding social order" (Nisbet, 1971:1). In this view, the acid test of a social problem is not its severity or magnitude but its undesirability to substantial numbers of persons.

The public opinion paradigm tells the researcher to investigate conditions considered objectionable by many people. For the knowledge-values paradigm, this information is useful though insufficient and possibly misleading. What is most important about social problems is their demonstrable seriousness. Thus, our paradigms channel our definitions and their consequences.

Concepts are specific definitions. What may seem to be a slight change in definition can produce substantially different findings. "If the line that determines poverty were lowered as little as one hundred dollars a year, millions of people previously defined as poor would no longer be poor, even though not a single remediable step had been taken" (Reissman, 1972:8). Calculating the magnitude of poverty calls for suitable indicators of its severity.

As precise definitions of situations or behavior, concepts are guides for scientific inquiry. They are essential elements of research hypotheses. An *hypothesis* is merely an untested but testable statement. For example, we have hypothesized that racial discrimination leads to black unemployment. Some consider this to be a *fact* or an empirically confirmed hypothesis.

Hypotheses may be derived from *theories*, that is, interrelated sets of propositions. Based on the general propositions of the differential association theory, we hypothesize that boys whose best friends engage in delinquent acts will tend to do likewise. Hypotheses can also be developed from observations and can serve to produce new, more comprehensive propositions.

The basic concepts of the knowledge-values paradigm are concerned with the identification and analysis of objectively detrimental conditions. They suggest propositions about the actual seriousness of social problems. Clarifying the relationships between magnitude, severity, and primacy is part of the unfinished business of explaining social problems.

What we look for is guided by our paradigms, their concepts, hypotheses, and theories. What we find is *data*, information obtained for research purposes. The validity of our data depends upon the quality of our research efforts.

By *validity* is meant the correspondence between concepts or statements and data. A valid research instrument is one that accurately measures what it is supposed to measure. A thermometer should show actual changes in temperature. A questionnaire should (but doesn't always) reveal what it is designed to find. Police reports, to take a negative example, have limited validity as measures of the true magnitude of crime.

The *reliability* of a research technique means its consistency and dependability. A reliable technique produces the same results under the same conditions. The reliability of survey respondents can be checked by asking similar questions. Although high reliability does not establish validity, low reliability is discrediting.

Another way of testing validity is to compare the findings produced by a research technique with those of other research techniques. The use of multiple research methods has been called *triangulation* (Denzin, 1970:26). Official reports of rates of crime, mental disorders, or housing discrimination can be compared with the estimates of knowledgeable experts. Surveys in selected areas can disclose respondents' personal experience with such problems.

Collecting accurate data about social problems is time-consuming and costly. Sampling methods simplify the research task. As a publisher is said to have replied to a rejected and complaining writer, "You don't have to eat the whole egg to find out that it's rotten." A representative sample is a good substitute for the whole thing.

A commonly used method to achieve representativeness is *random sampling*, "a procedure that provides an equal opportunity of selection to each unit in the population" (Mueller et al., 1970:362). Drawing names scrambled in a container is a simple form of random sampling. Tables of random numbers are available aids for sampling numbered cases (1970:452–54).

Data concerning a truly random sample of a prison population can be generalized to characterize the larger group from which it is drawn. The data, however, will *not* be representative of the entire criminal population. The uncaught or unconvicted law violators who have been omitted might be smarter, be more expert, or have enough money for better lawyers. Most of our information about criminals, however, comes from studies of convicted offenders.

Data Analysis

You may have heard the saying, "Garbage in, garbage out." Computer users are reminded by GIGO that poor data input results in poor output. Interpretation requires satisfactory data. It also requires good methods of analysis. We shall deal with some basic ways of analyzing information about social problems. Later sections will describe some of the important methods of data collection and interpretation.

A simple way of describing the magnitude of a social problem is to add together all the known cases. The poverty population can be said to consist of the total number of persons whose income falls below a predetermined level. The magnitude of crime, alcoholism, or mental disorders can be summarized similarly. I shall describe four types of measurements, or scales, appropriate to the magnitude and severity of social problems.

Simple addition is appropriate *if* each unit is essentially comparable. Using a ruler to measure length in inches assumes that each inch-mark covers the same distance. Our measurement of costs relies on currencies with equal-interval differences. Every dollar is worth one hundred cents. Equal-interval, or *interval scales,* are based on comparable units, such as income, in defining poverty levels.

Social data are seldom so uniform. Official reports of the magnitude of crime include many different kinds of law violations. Some crimes involve property, such as burglary. Assault, on the other hand, is a crime against persons. Measurements of the magnitude of all crimes take the form of a *nominal scale.*

The categories that are combined in a nominal scale are qualitatively different. "Nominal scales are scales in name only" (Mueller, *et al.,* 1970:15). They can be added like apples, oranges, and bananas. These, as with alcoholism or mental disorders, include somewhat similar units. Though each unit is not equivalent or interchangeable, enumeration is proper—with caution.

An *ordinal scale* is a measurement based on a rank order. For instance, psychiatrists diagnose cases of mental disorders as mild, moderate, or severe. The categories form a rank order of severity. Each case can be measured on an ordinal scale by giving each a score—perhaps of 1, 2, or 3 points. By adding individual scores together, we can produce an indicator of the severity of mental disorder within a group or community.

Another example of ordinal measurement is the ranking of the severity of crimes. The FBI category of Crime Index Offenses includes homicide, rape, and burglary. These could be ranked also in terms of severity. By comparison, vagrancy and loitering violations are minor or trivial offenses. A rank order of crimes based on their harmfulness is an ordinal scaling of severity.

The last type of measurement to be discussed is that of *ratio scales.* The latter is used "when there is some way of showing how many *times* greater one object is than another" (Green, 1954:337). Ratio scales are useful for comparing the magnitude of different social problems. Earlier, we cited statistics on the amounts of traffic fatalities and of homicides. Their ratio of five to one is a precise way of comparing their magnitude.

Ratio scales have been used to compare the perceived seriousness of social problems. An illustration is the rating of juvenile acts. In one study, a number of persons were asked to estimate the seriousness of these offenses (Sellin and Wolfgang, 1964:268). These judgments were used to compare perceptions of harmfulness.

On the basis of the judgments, the authors developed indexes of the harmfulness of various juvenile offenses. Not surprisingly, homicide was rated far more harmful than all other offenses. By multiplying the actual occurrence of specific delinquencies and the harmfulness scores, they arrived at measures of "community harm," "average offender seriousness," and similar indicators of seriousness.

These methods of measurement are especially useful for specifying the magnitude and severity of social problems. For their primacy, we need to investigate cause-effect relationships. These relationships can be tested through correlation methods. *Correlation* means covariation, the degree to which different entities are associated.

An example is the connection between income and

health care. Poor people are less apt to have adequate nutrition, medication, and physician contact than more affluent persons. Another is the relationship between income and education. High school dropouts are more frequent among the poor, college attendance among the more affluent.

A common measure of the relationship between variables is the *coefficient of correlation.* The coefficient is a calculation that usually produces figures ranging from +1.0 through zero to –1.0. Positive numbers show that the variables increase or decrease together, as income and college attendance. Negative numbers tell us that they vary inversely, as one increases the other decreases. The rate of dropouts decreases as income increases.

Correlation does not confirm causation. The absence of correlation, however, is disconfirming. Evidence of correlation is a first step in the effort to make inferences of causation. Generally, our next step is to examine *control variables,* other factors that may be responsible for the correlation.

In an experiment we can control environmental factors, such as the size of the groups or the type of activity. We can assign similar or matched individuals to control and experimental groups. For example, to control the influence of income in an experiment, we may use only middle-income subjects.

Most sociological researches are not experimental. Our information about discrimination and crime may be influenced by differences in people's income, education, or marital status. Hence, we compare the relationships between discrimination and crime within different income or educational levels. If our correlations disappear or sharply decrease, we can assume that the other factors are apt to be responsible for the original correlation.

Confirmed correlations strengthen our inferences of causation. Our final step is to decide their *causal direction* (Stinchcombe, 1968:34). That is, we want to know which condition is cause and which is effect. In experiments, we can manipulate the conditions in order to uncover causal direction.

Another way is to examine their logical or empirical time-sequence. A cause cannot follow an effect. An obvious illustration might be the correlation between levels of auto speeds and rates of traffic fatalities. We expect the former to precede the latter and not vice versa.

Scientific caution and philosophical issues over causal analysis have fostered a substitute terminology. Sociologists often use *independent variable* rather than cause, *dependent variable* in place of effect. I shall use these paired terms interchangeably.

Knowledge of data collection and analysis is needed for understanding social problems. We need to know how specific methods are used, what they reveal, and what they neglect. The remaining sections will describe some of the commonly used methods appropriate for studying social problems.

Social Records

A research manual asserts that "the measurement systems used by sociologists receive their most intensive use when applied to data generated by modern bureaucracies. . . . Most of the data that sociologists honor as 'given,' therefore, are largely the product of bureaucratically organized activities, for example, census bureaus, vital statistics bureaus, correctional agencies, welfare agencies, and business agencies" (Cicourel, 1964:36). By *social records,* I mean the information compiled for organizational purposes.

Many of our interpretations about the magnitude of crime, family problems, unemployment, poverty, and other social problems are secondhand. Analyses of their severity and primacy are based on these data. Their completeness and their validity are critical for determining the seriousness of social problems.

Record-keeping procedures of the public and private agencies of society have been explored by the techniques of *ethnomethodology*. The term has been applied to studies of the "practical reasoning" used by people in their everyday activities (Turner, 1974:7). It has been used to differentiate common sense and scientific thinking (Elliot, 1974:21). It has offered explanations of the records compiled by such organizations as hospitals, welfare agencies, and courts. An example is evidenced in the title of a research report, " 'Good' organizational reasons for 'bad' clinic records" (Garfinkel, 1967:186).

Before taking up the shortcomings of social records, it is proper that I present a summary of their advantages. First, there are far too many social problems to limit their study to sociologists. Second, the staffs of social organizations have technical knowledge and experience relevant to their social functions. Third, these organizations require the records and documentation both for public information and for their own effective operation. Fourth, their information can be evaluated and supplemented by other research methods.

Analyzing social problems requires appropriate concepts and methods. The basic difficulty with social records is their lack of congruence with sociological purposes. Though social scientists are employed by various social organizations, their obligation is to serve those employers. Other bureaucrats may be less trained and more concerned with job security than scientific or public knowledge.

Concepts deemed appropriate for a society or its institutions can be inappropriate or misleading for sociological analyses. The categories of juvenile delinquency are illustrative of exaggerated magnitude.

"In the United States there are many behaviors which are not considered criminal if performed by an adult but which are defined as delinquent if committed by a juvenile. Thus, truancy and running away from home make up a large percentage of the United States' delinquency sta-

tistics. . . . In most European countries only the violation
of adult laws is considered delinquency. At the 1960
United Nations Conference in London, in order for the
United States to compare juvenile delinquency statistics
with those of other countries, it was necessary to eliminate this type of delinquent act—with the result that the
United States 'juvenile delinquency' rate dropped by 50
per cent" (Guttenberg, 1968:108–109).

An alternative deficiency of bureaucratic records is that
of omissions. Established institutions are not likely to doc-
ument conditions that raise doubts about either their benefits or that of their society. Police departments have
better records of blue-collar crime than of those committed by executives or by police officers. Public health officials keep records on disease and deaths; they do not
reveal information about the quality of physician services.

Governmental regulatory bureaus, at times, have been
charged with failure to report violations of consumer protection laws. According to the United Press on October
14, 1974, "In the 52 years that the present law has been
on the books, not one single price action has been brought
by the department [of agriculture] against a [milk] co-op."
On the basis of Agriculture Department records, there
has never been such a legal offense by a farmer cooperative.

Powerful individuals and groups are highly effective in
information control. The poor have less power—and we
know more about the problems they have and the problems they make. Data about wealth, power, price-fixing,
political manipulation, and white-collar crime are scarce
and insufficient. Basic structural problems of society are
not recorded regularly by established institutions. As a
result, we know least about the damage or harm of these
powerful structures. Social records concerning major social problems must be supplemented by other sources of
data.

Survey Methods

Despite the predominance of the public opinion definition of social problems, textbooks on social problems do not present any evidence of public concern to justify their selected topics. The lack of supportive data is remarkable, since sociologists have developed many of the techniques for obtaining this kind of information. Critics have contended that sociologists, usually, are overdependent on opinion and attitude surveys.

Surveys use interviews or questionnaires to obtain verbal information from target populations (Phillips, 1971:125). A familiar type is the national census conducted each decade in the United States since 1790. Begun mainly for governmental information, census records are used by social scientists, business, and industry. Sociologists also participate in census planning and analyses.

The basic data obtained by the census is *demographic,* information concerning such population characteristics as age, sex, race, marital status, occupation, and so on. Until 1970, the census was obtained through personal interviews in each household. Most of the 1970 census data were obtained by mailed questionnaires. Incomplete or unanswered questionnaires were followed with home interviews.

While the decennial census attempts to characterize the entire population of the nation, omissions do occur—especially of the poor, blacks, and migrants. The 1970 census of more than 203 million persons failed to reach an estimated 5 million persons. Intensive sample surveys are used to check the reliability and validity of other data sources. They are used also to obtain periodic information about unemployment and health problems.

Like other surveys, the census relies upon the perceptions and opinions of respondents. Erroneous or misleading responses can affect enumerations and their interpretation. The likelihood of error is greatest for sensitive information, such as income or personal problems. Thus, a follow-up study of family members of previously hospitalized mental patients found that 32 percent did not admit this treatment to interviewers (National Center for Health Statistics, 1965:25).

Opinions provide useful information about undesirable conditions. Opinion polls disclose public perceptions of social problems. The Gallup polls conducted over several decades showed that fears about war were common. In recent years, Watergate issues, inflation, and unemployment have been considered important social problems by many people.

A sample survey conducted in the city of Baltimore in 1972 offers information about perceptions of the seriousness of crimes (Rossi, Bose, Waite, and Berk, 1974). Respondents were asked to rate 140 different crimes on a scale of 1 to 9 points. The average score for each crime was then placed in a rank order to form a composite scale. The highest score, or most serious crime, was the planned killing of a policeman.

Least serious of the 140 offenses was being drunk in a public place. This finding is of interest, since the magnitude of public drunkenness is largest of all known offenses. Over a million arrests for this "crime" are reported yearly. Apparently, actual magnitude was not a factor in perceptions of drinking seriousness.

The reliability of official data can be tested by survey methods. The Bureau of the Census conducted sample surveys of crime rates in five large cities. Using interviews with large samples, the Bureau asked respondents to list crimes committed against them. According to the United Press (April 15, 1974), the findings revealed high rates of unreported crimes known to the respondents.

The ratio of unreported to reported crimes ranged from about two to one for New York to about five to one for Philadelphia. The ratios were nearly three to one for

Chicago, Detroit, and Los Angeles. Whatever the validity of the survey data may be, the discrepancy between public perceptions and official records is critical for our appraisal of the magnitude of crimes.

One of the unresolved questions about survey research concerns the congruence between verbal statements about behavior and the actual behaviors (see Deutscher, 1973). Interviews and questionnaires tell us what people believe or what they want us to believe about them. Studies, too numerous to mention here, show conflicting levels of agreement between verbal reports and actions (Liska, 1974).

Survey researches aid in explaining what people say, think, and feel. Surveys are useful in revealing perceptions of undesirable conditions. They are helpful in predicting what individuals and groups will do. They can disclose deficiencies in other sources of information. They are efficient and relatively economical ways of obtaining data. However, surveys are but one among many research techniques.

Observation

Are sociologists nosy intruders in the private lives of their subjects? If asking questions for surveys is implied, the answer is yes. An analysis of articles published in two leading sociological journals during 1965–1966 showed that 92 percent were based on interviews, questionnaires, or both (Brown and Gilmartin, 1969:287). Only 8 percent of the articles used actual observation. Sociologists listen to people's opinions; they seldom watch what people do.

One reason for the limited use of observational techniques is their difficulty. It is much easier and less costly to ask questions about behaviors than to observe them. Another reason is the possible risks. Observing theft or family quarrels can be physically or legally dangerous.

Still another reason is values. Sociologists are concerned

increasingly over the ethics of research, in particular of disguised observation. The suggestion has been made that "it is unethical for a sociologist to *deliberately misrepresent* his identity for the purpose of entering a private domain *to which he is not otherwise eligible*" (Erikson, 1967:373). Guarding the privacy and integrity of group members is a social responsibility of science.

Techniques of observation differ. What is used must be suitable to the research topic and to the skills of the researcher. The options range from the high involvement of participant observation to more impersonal and indirect methods of observation.

Participant observation is intensive, intimate involvement by the researcher in the social processes that are being studied. The basic principle has been described in the following statement: "The participant observer shares in the life activities and sentiments of people in face-to-face relationships" (Bruyn, 1966:13). By experiencing the behavior and subjective feelings of the other participants, the researcher expects to grasp the nature and meaning of their activity.

The degree of involvement in participant observation can be varied. Total involvement may be difficult, if not impossible or illegal. This limit is especially true for studies of deviant behavior. As a practitioner of the technique with criminals has noted, "Participant observation does not necessarily entail 'participating' with the subjects in all their activities" (Irwin, 1972:118). That is welcome advice for dedicated though law-abiding researchers.

Through participant observation, the researcher can develop the rapport and the trust of group members. The outcome is improved insight into their motivations, relationships, and social problems. Usually, the sought-for data are *qualitative,* rather than quantitative. For example, *Tally's Corner,* a much-praised, award-winning book on black street-corner men contains no numerical data (Liebow, 1967). What it does is carefully describe and explain their dreary living quarters, irregular and low-paid jobs, fights, friendships, and family troubles.

Observation does not require full participation or involvement by the researcher. The observer can choose detachment and non-involvement in recording actions or events. One such study revealed the casual way in which individuals are committed to mental hospitals (Scheff, 1964).

The researchers attended more than a hundred judicial hearings for legal commitment of patients. Using criteria obtained by interview from the judges, they concluded that most were not legally "mentally ill." They found that the examiners had not recommended releasing *any* of the patients. They also noted that the average amount of time spent by the psychiatric examiners with the patients was about nine minutes.

The data obtained from these observations serve to challenge the established court practices through which individuals are committed to mental hospitals. They raise doubts about the label of mental illness. They also dispute the validity of official records on the magnitude of the problem.

Obtaining access to psychiatric examinations is not always possible. Where access is difficult or close observation is disruptive, less direct procedures of observation are applicable. These have been called *non-reactive research* by the authors of a volume on the subject (Webb, Campbell, Schwartz, and Sechrest, 1966). The resulting data are *unobtrusive measures* of social phenomena.

Their first example concerns the floor tiles around a hatching-chick exhibit at a museum. The floor tiles are replaced every six weeks. Elsewhere in the museum, they last for years. The erosion of tiles shows the observer the relative popularity or unpopularity of the exhibits.

In addition to observable, physical traces of behavior, there are other unobtrusive measures. They suggest a more systematic, critical use of commercial and governmental records. My own illustration would be the use of gun or door-lock sales as indicators of the extent of fears about crime.

Comparative Studies

With a few notable exceptions (Eisenstadt, 1964; Kavolis, 1969; Kinch, 1974), books and articles on social problems deal mainly with conditions in the United States. There have been thousands of studies by anthropologists, psychologists, and sociologists that could loosely be called comparative. The field of *comparative sociology* applies to "the systematic and explicit comparison of data from two or more societies" (Marsh, 1967:11).

Among the early cross-national comparisons of social problems was the 1899 publication on suicide by Durkheim. As I mentioned in Chapter 1, Durkheim tried to uncover the causes of suicide. His data were obtained from official reports of European countries (1951:47). He found that the magnitude of suicides tended to remain stable in each society over the years. Anomie was one of his explanations.

A more current example is a comparative study of the relationship between military spending and economic stagnation (Szymanski, 1973). The author obtained information concerning 18 countries from such sources as the United Nations *Statistical Yearbook*. Using correlation coefficients, he found that increased military expenditures were associated with reduced unemployment but were less influential in reducing economic stagnation.

We have seen that official data vary in their reliability and validity. In different countries, differing criteria are used to define undesirable conditions. My prior reference to the great differences in the magnitude of delinquency in the United States as compared to other countries is illustrative. Comparative analyses require careful examination of the conceptions and data-collection methods used in each society.

Some official records, such as industrial production and birth and death rates, are fairly uniform, especially among the more affluent, modernized societies. Using official data from 25 countries, deLint (1975) calculated rates of excessive alcohol consumption. His criterion of excessive usage was set at a daily average, per person, of more than 15 centiliters of absolute alcohol. The highest rate of excessive alcohol users was attributed to France: about 11 out of every 100 persons aged 15 and over. The United States was ranked fourteenth with about two excessive drinkers per 100 persons.

The "health damage" of excessive alcohol consumption was also reviewed by deLint. Summarizing seven studies conducted in five different countries, he found that excessive users of alcohol had death rates from two to nearly four times higher than the normal rates. Such comparisons help to clarify the actual magnitude and severity of alcohol problems.

Comparative studies using survey or observational methods are more costly and more difficult than those using official published information. Conducting research in several societies is expensive, entailing much travel and communication. Cultural barriers compound the difficulties.

The multiplicity of world languages is an obvious barrier to comparative research. Few sociologists are multilingual. Even those who are must rely on the cooperation of other sociologists and informants. Establishing rapport with interviewees is especially challenging.

As alien outsiders, sociologists may be objects of suspicion and distrust. Foreign governments often perceive or imagine risks in research by visiting scholars. These fears are magnified when the research concerns social problems. Studies of poverty may arouse misgivings over possible subversion or of espionage. Research on mental illness, family problems, or crime, when conducted by foreign sociologists, may seem to threaten national pride.

Examining studies by different investigators in their own countries can facilitate comparative analysis of social problems. The review of studies of alcohol damage in various countries that were described by deLint (cited above) is a case in point. At times, however, the comparisons reveal the distorting influences of incompatible definitions and research techniques upon problem identification. An illustration is the enormous variation in reported rates of mental illness by different investigators located throughout the world.

In a review of researches on "psychological disorders," Dohrenwend and Dohrenwend (1969) summarized the findings of 44 different investigations throughout the world. They found that the reported rates of persons with psychological disorders ranged from less than one percent to 64 percent within different groups. Although the lowest rates occurred in several Asian communities, rates as low as one and two percent were reported in some European and North American communities. The highest rate of psychological disorders was claimed for a small Canadian fishing village. Studies made in the United States showed rates as low as two percent and as high as 30 percent.

It is possible, of course, that the variations in the findings reflect true national or local differences in the magnitude of mental disorders. Another possibility is that the differences in rates of disorders were produced by heterogeneous research techniques. They may also be a result of inconsistent criteria of what is "normal" and what is not. These discrepancies in international comparisons focus attention on our ways of interpreting and evaluating social conditions.

Comparative studies of values have been suggested in order to produce cross-national criteria for identifying and assessing social problems. A noted philosopher arranged to have a questionnaire dealing with values sent to male college students in six countries (Morris, 1956).

These were: Canada, India, Japan, Norway, Taiwan, and the United States.

Using factor analysis (a correlational technique), he compared the preferred values of the six sets of samples. Of especial interest were the findings about the American students. They scored highest on values related to self-indulgence and self-orientation. They were lowest on sympathetic concern for others and for self-control. The Canadian students had scores very much like those of the United States students.

The above-reported values of students in the United States resemble those assumed to have been prevalent in the past. These have been preferences for "rugged individualism," independence, free enterprise, and the like. Student activism in the 1960s suggests that students in that period have been more socially conscious and involved (Flacks, 1971). Comparative study of national differences in attitudes toward problem solutions would be helpful.

Evaluation Research

Some sociologists separate *pure* from *applied* research (see Gouldner and Miller, 1965). Pure research is aimed primarily at advancing sociological knowledge. Applied research is assumed to be limited to practical applications. Both use similar techniques of data collection and analysis. Their difference lies in their purposes.

Inspection of research reports in major professional journals reveals that many have little immediate or practical usefulness. Others even seem to make scant contributions to theoretical knowledge. Still, they obviously differ from studies designed to improve product sales, worker satisfactions, or prisoner rehabilitation.

An important product of applied research has been the development of techniques of evaluation. In studying programs that deal with social problems, researchers have had to grapple directly with the question of values. For the most part, their researches drew upon the explicit or implicit values of their employers or their funding sources.

Evaluation research is the appraisal of the outcomes of social actions (see Rossi and Williams, 1972). Usually, such research seeks to learn about the effectiveness of programs or organizations. A major stimulus to evaluation research was the 1960 War on Poverty. Questions about program successes and failures led to requests for their appraisal. The economists' model of cost-benefit analyses has frequently guided research procedures.

Another influence has been public pressures for accountability, particularly of the schools. By *accountability* is meant the disclosure of the usefulness of social institutions. Taxpayers, parents, and students demand increasingly that the high costs of education result in acceptable levels of learning.

Examinations are a familiar, traditional way of appraising student performance. More recent are evaluations by students of their courses and instructors. Some of the studies contradict accepted beliefs about learning. One study reported that class size had little effect on actual course evaluations (Jiobu and Pollis, 1971:319). Another finding was that students believed they learned more in courses where their instructors were less tolerant of disagreements. Some instructors (including myself) will doubt the accuracy of such perceptions.

The so-called "Coleman report" is an example of large-scale evaluation (Coleman, et al., 1966). The research was commissioned by the United States Office of Education in accordance with the Civil Rights Act of 1964. It was designed to investigate educational opportunities of minority children—racial, ethnic, and religious.

Nearly 600,000 pupils completed questionnaires about their educational aspirations and home life. They also took ability and achievement tests. Information was obtained about teacher training, attitudes, and abilities and about school facilities, curricula, and administration. About 20,-000 teachers, principals, and administrators participated in the project.

Not surprisingly, the study found extensive racial segregation in the schools. The study also showed great differences in the average achievement scores of the various minority groups. On the verbal test, as well as the other tests, the average scores of white students were higher than those of all the rest. Lowest averages were achieved by the black students.

The most controversial conclusions were drawn from information concerning the schools. Except for segregated versus unsegregated schools, the data showed little differences between schools in student performance. The authors asserted, therefore, that home and neighborhood were much more important than schools in influencing achievement by students. Although the research design and the interpretations have been attacked, the findings parallel those reported by other investigators (Sewell and Armer, 1966).

A frequent criticism of evaluation researches is their excessive reliance upon quantitative measures of success and failure. Outcomes that cannot be measured in numbers are apt to be ignored. Complex situations may be oversimplified. Readily available data can lead to major evaluation errors.

Where cost-benefit evaluation is sought, economic values dominate conclusions. Financial considerations are important and more easily measured. Dollars spent and saved can be enumerated better than degrees of human dignity or social well-being.

Some forms of social data are available in quantitative form. Among them are statistical information concerning health, safety, social participation, and the environment.

Compilations of these data have been used as social indicators appropriate for evaluation research and for guiding public policy. *Social indicators* are measurements of community or society well-being. They permit evaluation of the quality of life in a nation or in a city.

An example is *Toward a Social Report*, produced by the U.S. Department of Health, Education, and Welfare (1970). The report asked such questions as, are we becoming healthier? and, how much opportunity is there? Data were obtained from governmental and private sources. Presented as social indicators of health and mobility, the report produced generally favorable conclusions about conditions in the United States.

Social problems indicators (Guttman, 1971) are measurements of harmful conditions. They apply to data concerning poverty, crime, racial conflict, and the like. Many social indicators are available on the magnitude and severity of social problems. For instance, one study of eighteen metropolitan areas located and compiled information about unemployment, poverty, robberies, and suicide (Flax, 1972). St. Louis had the highest poverty rates; Chicago, the highest infant mortality rates, and Cleveland, the highest rates of unemployment.

Thomas Jefferson once said that the purpose of all knowledge is action. I believe that his position denies the intrinsic values of knowledge. The search for improved understanding is itself satisfying and worthwhile. Improving the level of individual and public awareness is an important responsibility of science.

Our serious social problems, however, do require action as well as understanding. For all our technological advances, we have done little to solve the problems of war, of overpopulation, of racism, and of individuals troubled by mental disorder or alcoholism. We need to apply our knowledge toward the prevention and the solution of our social problems.

Summary

My aim in this chapter has been to suggest ways for distinguishing between minor or unimportant social problems and more critical ones. I have used the term perceived seriousness of social problems to describe the beliefs of group members about the harmfulness of social phenomena. These views must not be confused with the demonstrable seriousness of social problems—the degree to which objectively determined conditions are detrimental to human well-being.

I have described three aspects of seriousness: (1) the magnitude of social problems refers to the amount or extent of the conditions; (2) severity is applied to the degree of actual harmfulness of social problems; (3) primacy concerns the level or multiplicity of their causal consequences. The latter includes primary, secondary, and tertiary social problems.

Accurate data and careful analyses are needed for assessing the seriousness of social problems. The validity of our data concerns their congruence with our concepts and propositions. Reliable techniques are those that produce the same techniques under the same conditions. Measurements may take the form of interval, nominal, ordinal, and ratio scales. Coefficients of correlation specify the extent to which variables are interrelated.

Much of our data about social problems come from information compiled by organizations—social records. Also, sociologists often use questionnaires and interviews in their survey researches. Observational data can be very valuable but are very difficult to obtain. These techniques may be used in comparative research, such as studies conducted in different countries. A recent development is evaluation research, which attempts to appraise action programs.

The final chapter deals with the prevention and solution of social problems. In it, I shall discuss the application of scientific knowledge-values for solving problems, as well as the limitations of science. Earlier conceptions of societal problem solving will be reviewed. A special concern will be the kind of society that promotes structural efforts aimed at improving social conditions.

RECOMMENDED READING

Babbie, Earl R. *Survey Research Methods.* Belmont, Calif.: Wadsworth, 1973. A source useful for descriptions of questionnaire construction, interviewing, sampling, and other survey methods.

Coleman, James S., et al *Equality of Educational Opportunity.* Washington, D.C.: U.S. Government Printing Office, 1966. Available in paperback, this comprehensive report aroused great national interest and controversy.

Douglas, Jack D., ed. *Research on Deviance.* New York: Random House, 1972. A reader with clear, well-written articles on observational techniques used in studying deviant behavior.

Durkheim, Emile. *Suicide.* Glencoe, Ill.: Free Press, 1951. An English translation of the classic 1899 research by a noted French sociologist. It is important not only for its report on the magnitude of suicide in European countries but also for its theory of causation.

Erikson, Kai T. *Wayward Puritans.* New York: John Wiley, 1966. This study of deviant behavior focused upon the social perceptions that led to witch-hunts and a variety of severe penalties.

Federal Bureau of Investigation. *Uniform Crime Reports.* Washington, D.C.: U.S. Government Printing Office. An annual bulletin summarizing data from local police records.

Flax, Michael J. *A Study in Comparative Urban Indicators: Conditions in Large Metropolitan Areas.* Washington, D.C.: The Urban Institute, 1972. A monograph applies the social indicator method to compare conditions in large cities.

Gans, Herbert J. "The Positive Functions of Poverty." *American Journal of Sociology* 78 (September 1972): 275–289. One of the few attempts to examine the social benefits of social problems. It helps to explain why some social problems are not prevented or solved.

Gouldner, Alvin W., and S. M. Miller, eds. *Applied Sociology: Opportunities and Problems.* New York: Free Press, 1965. A collection of useful articles dealing with practical applications of sociological methods and knowledge.

Manis, Jerome G. "Assessing the Seriousness of Social Problems." *Social Problems* 22 (October 1974): 1–15. Recommended for its obvious pertinence to this chapter.

Marsh, Robert M. *Comparative Sociology.* New York: Harcourt, Brace and World, 1967. A description of the methods, difficulties, and prospects of comparative research. In addition to summaries of specific researches, the book contains a bibliography of more than a thousand studies.

Miller, Delbert C. *Handbook of Research Design and Measurement.* New York: David McKay, 1970. This is a manual with brief descriptions of basic research techniques and many examples of scales used to measure social phenomena.

Rossi, Peter H., and Walter Williams, eds. *Evaluating Social Programs.* New York: Seminar Press, 1972. The articles in this book illustrate the theory, methods, and controversies of evaluation research.

United States Bureau of the Census. *Statistical Abstract of the United States.* Washington, D.C.: U.S. Government Printing Office. Published yearly, each volume contains data on crime, illness, employment, and many other topics. Very helpful for term papers.

United States Department of Health, Education, and Welfare. *Toward a Social Report.* Ann Arbor, Mich.: University of Michigan Press, 1970. A state-of-the-nation report using available social indicators. Since complex conditions were identified by single or simple indicators, the findings should be used with caution.

5
Prevention and Solution

"A social problem exists when many people believe it exists. To prevent or solve social problems, we should persuade people that they don't exist." Who said this? I did—and not merely to appear witty. This so-called solution is one possible inference from the public opinion paradigm.

The early contributors to the paradigm were optimistic about solutions to social problems. As we saw in Chapter 1, Fuller and Myers believed that social problems have a natural history; first comes awareness of an undesirable condition; then public debate over possible solutions; finally, the achievement of reform. How unrecognized or potential problems could be prevented received scant attention.

Optimism about our problem-solving abilities reached a high point during the early 1960s, as was manifest in the civil rights legislation, poverty programs, and educational reforms of the period. Dissatisfaction with their outcomes has been accompanied by the new problems of food and energy shortages, unemployment, and inflation. Pessimism is the theme of the 1970s.

Some writers assert that excessive expectations were

responsible for the violence of the latter part of the 1960s. "By the end of 1968, public frustration and social tensions in the United States had reached a dangerous level. Americans demanded a quantity and variety of social improvements far beyond the capacity of this or any other society to produce (Jacoby, 1971:39).

In Jacoby's view, the concerns of the public led not to solutions but to new difficulties—frustrations, tensions, and "irrelevant protest." The interpretation contains a basic inconsistency. While the public is said to define what a social problem is, the author sits in final judgment; that is, he decides what is relevant or irrelevant protest. Let us look at his definition and his proposed solution.

To Jacoby, a social problem is "a gap between public expectations of social conditions and social realities" (1971:39). He is critical of politicians and mass media that emphasize or exaggerate harmful conditions (Advocates of the public opinion definition tend to ignore these influences.) He recommends that our political leaders "should keep the gap at a tolerable size." In other words, the public provides the criteria of social problems, but its leaders should control public opinion.

I have argued that popular concerns can be aroused by spurious or trivial social problems. I believe that a responsibility of sociologists is to inform their society about such misconceptions. We should also be responsible for informing society about barriers to solving real problems. We must admit the deficiencies in our knowledge and point out the limitations of our resources. However, reducing public concerns over serious problems is unethical, whether practiced by scientists or by political elites.

Viewing science as public knowledge can help to improve the quality of public opinion. The knowledge-values of science urge accurate disclosure of information about social problems. Of special importance is the disclosure of the values that guide scientific theories and methods.

Applying Knowledge-Values

Before considering ways to prevent or solve social problems, we need to decide where we want to go. To say that
something is undesirable is to imply that something else
is preferable. I have suggested that the knowledge-values
of science—intrinsic, contextual, and social responsibility
—can provide sociologists with guidelines for studying
and appraising social problems. Such values are appropriate in specifying the nature and goals of social life.

As a writer on science policies has asserted, "Science is
universal by nature: the truths which scientists pursue are
not national truths; they are the same everywhere and
therefore can be universally recognized" (Salomon,
1973:209). A basic issue is whether these truth goals are
consistent with the needs of humanity.

In the past, some scientists have ignored the existence
of scientific values, assuming ethical neutrality to be the
only norm of the scientific enterprise. Now, however,
there is increasingly evidence that scientists are identifying the value premises of science. Also on the increase is
opposition to the uses of science for purposes detrimental
to humanity. These concerns have led to efforts at specifying the proper values of science.

We have seen, in Chapter 2, that scientists and philosophers are exploring a scientific basis for human values.
Opponents claim that this is impossible. "Many minds
have sought a scientific basis for ethics, in this century as
in many others. The effort is doomed to failure, not because of the limitations of the human mind but because,
by definition, science and ethics are two different kinds of
enterprises and two different kinds of inquiries" (Bierstedt, 1965:413).

Whether or not these efforts are doomed by definition
to failure remains to be seen. The outcome will be decided neither by grandiose claims nor by doomsday
prophecies. The test will be the quality of our efforts and
their social practicality.

A French molecular biologist has pointed out "... the moral contradictions which menace modern societies. They have accepted to reap the fruits of science. They have not accepted, hardly have they understood, the ethics of knowledge upon which science is based. Yet this ethic is the only one able to lay the foundations of a value system wholly compatible with science itself and able to serve humanity in its 'scientific age' " (Monod, 1972:16). To state and to suggest these values to society is a crucial task of science.

Scientific knowledge has advanced most in satisfying our material wants—communication, transportation, energy, subsistence, and the like. Our greatest need is to prevent and overcome our social problems—war, poverty, racism, and family and personal troubles. A major barrier is the belief that science cannot help in deciding what is good or bad.

The knowledge-values of science are appropriate ways of defining, studying, and controlling social problems. They are based on the experiences of a worldwide community of truth-seekers and correspond with our best understanding of nature and humanity.

Unlike other organisms, human beings need not respond blindly to environmental conditions. Through their ability to use symbols, they are able to interpret their experiences. Culture is the accumulation and communication of traditional patterns of human behavior. In the past, these were products of trial- and-error learning.

Science has emerged from humanity's symbolic-cultural capabilities. As a founder of symbolic interactionism has put it, "the scientific method is, after all, only the evolutionary process grown self-conscious" (Mead, 1956:23). Intentional discovery and innovation are among the goals of science.

In modern societies, science has become a basis of social change. According to a leading scientist, what is most important about science is that "it is a major source of man's dissatisfaction with the world as it is. It is a wellspring of man's discontent with the status quo" (Roberts, 1971:12). However, we need to recognize the limits as well as the potential benefits of scientific knowledge.

The Limitations of Scientific Knowledge

The existence of problems does not lead automatically to their solution. Advocates of the public opinion paradigm have been overly optimistic about the possibility of solutions to social problems. Proposing the application of the knowledge-values of science does not guarantee their solution.

A fundamental barrier to problem-solving is the diversity of human values. Although science is universal and cross-national, cultures are many and different. Communism is valued in Soviet Russia but is considered a problem in the United States. To many Catholics, abortion is a harmful problem; to many others, it is a solution.

The knowledge-values of science need to be fitted to the needs of humanity. The great variety of individual and societal characteristics raises great difficulties. Problem-defining and problem-solving must consider these important differences.

Scientists should not, and will not, be permitted to impose their knowledge and values on others. A sociologist who has studied the scientific community stated that " 'art for art's sake' and 'knowledge as an end in itself' are still advanced as slogans when other groups in society no longer dare express such similar views as 'the public be damned' " (Hagstrom, 1965:295). Recognizing the diversity of human values is required of science.

A second, related limitation concerns the applications of scientific knowledge. If science is public knowledge, its usage also belongs in the hands of the world society. Science seeks to know and, I would suggest, to inform but not to control.

Science is said to be disinterested, not used for private gain. However true this may be, people must view with great concern any group with great power. It has been said that power corrupts and absolute power corrupts absolutely (Acton, 1962:365). Since knowledge is power, those who possess it may be tempted to extend and use it for their own purposes.

As members of society, we have reason to fear those who would control us for our own good. In maintaining social order, force is used to protect group members against harm, such as burglary or homicide. Reaching an acceptable balance between individual freedom and social order is difficult. No elite of church or state, of military or science can be expected to offer satisfactory answers to every unanswered question.

The third limitation is concerned with the deficiencies of social knowledge. There are numerous gaps in our understanding of human behavior and groups. The social sciences have much reason to be modest in their claims. Specific solutions for some social problems, at the present time, will need to be tentative and be considered cautiously.

The variety of social problems paradigms is evidence of our inadequacies. Sociology contains a number of competing theoretical perspectives. There are controversies over the definitions of our basic concepts—social class, roles, functions, and so on, and research studies have produced inconsistent or contradictory findings.

A current example is the continuing debate over the existence of a "culture of poverty" (see Della Fave, 1974). The term refers to a distinctive set of traditional beliefs and attitudes of the poor that prevent them from taking advantage of their opportunities for improvement. If true, it would help explain the persistence of poverty. However, numerous studies and analyses have resulted in opposite conclusions about its importance.

A fourth limitation grows out of the changeability of

social phenomena. The advances made in chemistry have been aided by the constancy of elements, and the stable orbits of planetary systems simplified the development of astronomy. But human behavior and institutions are far less stable.

From prehistoric to modern times, society and its members have changed tremendously, and the rate of change in the contemporary world has been accelerating. More innovations and inventions occur in a single year today than took place in prior centuries. New styles of dress, play, work, learning, and living appear and disappear in a moment.

Understanding or predicting social change is complicated by chance events. The assassination of a political leader, a major invention, or a new source of fuel can have unexpected, significant influences. The complexities of advanced societies add to the difficulties of social planning.

Whatever the limitations and difficulties, decisions must be made. We can allow our social problems to continue and to increase. We can act on the basis of tradition, of emotion, or of influences by powerful leaders. Better yet, we can seek to apply our best knowledge and techniques.

Our first step is to learn the lessons of experience. Social problems have existed in the past and so have attempted solutions. By examining these efforts, we can retain those that work, stop using those that don't, and consider alternative procedures. Let us examine sociological interpretations of group efforts at problem-solving.

Social Control

The public opinion paradigm defines social problems as behavior or conditions deemed undesirable by many members of a society. A related topic is the ways by which the society attempts to deter or limit undesirable social phenomena. One of the earliest conceptions by sociologists of these actions was social control, the topic of this section. A more recent concept, societal reaction, will be described in the next section.

Social control refers to society's techniques for maintaining social order by enforcing approved behavior. The term was emphasized by one of the founders of sociology, Edward A. Ross (1901), for whom, social control was necessary since human beings lacked the guidance of instincts.

Ross identified two types of *instruments of control.* The *ethical* controls were those imposed by religion, public opinion, and personal morality, and were exercised when the society's members were similar, equal, and cooperative. Under such circumstances, Ross contended, controls would be mild or moderate.

The stronger instruments of control were *political,* such as law and government, and were present where the groups in society were diverse, unequal, and in opposition. Ross' illustrations included regimentation, slavery, and racial subordination. The coercive controls benefit the more powerful group members.

It should be noted that Ross applied the term social control to the preservation of societal beliefs and values. Whether the controls benefit the few or the many, they deal with group perceptions of desirable or harmful behavior. In this sense, social control involves group attempts to prevent or solve what I have called "perceived social problems."

Sociologists continue to define social control as society's way of producing conformity to social norms (see Dressler and Carns, 1973:116; Mirande, 1975:18). The process by which individuals acquire and internalize norms is called "socialization," which is accomplished through the important agencies of the family, church, and school.

My point in this discussion is that the forms of social control support established or powerful ideas and practices. By definition, social controls aim at achieving stability, consensus and conformity. Unless our social institutions encourage appraisal of their objectively harmful characteristics, social control can only mean the continuation of accepted conditions.

An extreme method of social control is the death penalty for norm violators. Execution has been assumed to be a technique for halting serious crimes. It is believed to deter others as well as killing the offender. Ignoring the question of its ethical implications, let us consider its usages and consequences.

A specialist in law and philosophy has compiled a useful anthology of studies on the death penalty (Bedau, 1964). According to Bedau, there were more than 200 types of crime punishable by death in Britain as late as 1819. The Massachusetts Bay Colony used capital punishment for such offenses as idolatry, witchcraft, blasphemy, sodomy, rape, and murder. How effective and desirable these penalties have been is questionable.

We know much more about the effects of the death penalty in the United States. A comparison of states that abolished the death penalty and those that retain it is instructive. A number of studies have shown that the total of all murder rates, the killing of local police officers, and the killing of state policemen are unaffected by the presence or absence of capital punishment for these offenses. States that abolished the death penalty have not had increased homicides, and states that reintroduced the death penalty have not lowered their homicide rates (cited in Bedau, 1964:chs. IV and V).

The investigations show that the death penalty does not prevent or solve the problem of homicide. Most killings are committed by family members or acquaintances of the victims, and most killers use weapons that are easily available in the United States. A former attorney general of the United States correlated homicide rates with the prevalence of guns (Clark, 1971:82ff.) and reported the highest rates of homicide in states where gun controls are lax and gun ownership is common. Controlling guns, it would seem, is a far more effective method of reducing homicide rates than capital punishment.

Imprisonment is a more common method of social control. Although, like the death penalty a form of punishment, a prison term is supposed to rehabilitate the offender as well as to deter others from violating the law. But the success of imprisonment in achieving these aims has been limited.

The modern prison has been described as a product of American innovations (Rothman, 1971). During the early nineteenth century, people became concerned about the prevalence of crime, insanity, and poverty, the causes of which were believed to be lack of religious training, wicked parents, and evil friends. Removing individuals from these corrupt influences was suggested as the proper solution by public officials, legislators, and philanthropists.

Thus, new institutions were constructed to isolate and change the criminal, the delinquent, the insane, and the pauper. Public optimism is revealed by the names given to these places: House of Refuge, House of Correction, Insane Asylum, Reformatory, and Penitentiary. Although the titles linger on, the optimism has faded away.

Evaluating the success of rehabilitation efforts by these institutions is difficult. As we have seen, official records are apt to be deceptive. An example is the insane asylum that claimed 274 recoveries (Rothman, 1971:131). The asylum had based its figures on only 87 inmates, one patient having been reported cured five times.

Studies often use the absence of new crime convictions as evidence of the success of prison rehabilitation. They have found that about three out of five convicted felons are not convicted for additional offenses over periods of four or five years (Tittle, 1974), but the figures do not include the large numbers of arrests that do not lead to convictions. They also omit unreported crimes.

Some criminologists assert that prisons train felons to be more successful at crime and evading arrest and conviction. They argue that prison experiences damage or toughen inmates (Ellis, Grasmick, and Gilman, 1974). Frequent contact with experienced criminals, homosexual rape, brutal treatment by other prisoners or by guards, and removal from family and community do little to reform the individual.

Social control has been a central assumption of traditional or classical criminology (see Taylor, Walton, and Young, 1973:2–3). From that viewpoint, criminal law was considered a product of social agreement or consensus. Its aims of punishment were believed necessary for protecting society against offenders. What is called social control, however, may have less desirable consequences. Other concepts, therefore, have been suggested by sociologists.

Societal Reaction

A major contributor to the deviance paradigm, Edwin M. Lemert (1951), introduced the term *societal reaction,* which refers to the ways people respond to behavior they consider undesirable. Although the definition resembles that of social control, societal reaction does not imply the prevention or solution of deviance. On the contrary, Lemert asserted that societal reactions often distort the effects of norm violations. At times, deviance may be tolerated or mildly penalized, while at other times, the reaction may be exaggerated.

To some sociologists, labeling is a basic form of societal reaction and deviant behavior a product of labeling. That is, what people believe to be undesirable results in placing a derogatory label on offenders, such as *homosexual, insane,* and *criminal.* In this sense, the "cause" of deviance is society's definitions, and passing more laws increases the potential for more violations.

The stigma of a deviant label may be imposed informally by members of a society. *Hippie, drunk, crazy,* or *bum* are traditional names for disapproved people, and when they are applied they may deter individuals from acting in socially unacceptable ways. They also make it difficult for persons so labeled to change or become accepted by others.

A *status degradation ceremony* is a formal action in which an individual or individuals are denounced and labeled as social offenders (Garfinkel, 1956). Through the ceremony, the public identity of the person is altered and lowered, as when a church assembly pronounces someone a heretic to be expelled and avoided. A criminal court action that results in conviction assigns the label of convict and the act of imprisonment.

Societal reactions to crime have varying relevance for crime prevention and solution. Court decisions are influenced by legal criteria of seriousness and of penalties; but they are also influenced by the power and status of the alleged offender (Nagel, 1968). Thus, white-collar offenses are less apt to be prosecuted than street crimes. In addition, wealthy suspects can purchase highly skilled legal services, and judges and juries tend to be more lenient with suspects of high social or political status.

Most crimes do not result in convictions and of those that do, about four out of five are "solved" by confessions (Skolnick, 1967:13). Confessions are often the product of negotiation between prosecutors and suspects. *Plea bargaining* usually involves confession to a lesser crime than the original charge. Under these circumstances, the societal reaction produces dubious criminal statistics and an irregular system of punishment. Prevention or solution of the problems of crime is almost irrelevant to the process.

The *new criminology* (Taylor, Walton, and Young, 1973), as it is being called, is reappraising established ideas and practices. Its advocates contend that societal reactions to deviance are often inappropriate and harmful. Noting the influences of power and inequality, they suggest the need for a value-oriented approach to crime, one based on the norms of equality, human diversity, and responsive social institutions.

A similar trend is evident among sociologists specializing in the study of mental illness. Here, too, an important influence has been researches on labeling and societal reactions. The label of mental illness is said to be applied after a minimum of examination (see Scheff, 1966). Moreover, commitment to a mental institution usually provides only limited treatment. Also critical is the lasting stigma of being mentally disordered.

The critics argue that behavior defined as mental illness is not a disease. They contend that the label diverts attention from the social influences upon behavior. The standards of mental illness are based on hidden values of conformity to traditional norms.

Contemporary reactions to deviance are based, increasingly, on a medical model of causation. From this perspective, the usual solutions are psychotherapy, drug therapy, and hospitalization. How good are these treatments? The answers vary.

Although most psychiatrists appear optimistic, others are doubtful (Szasz, 1961). Sociologists tend toward the latter view. As a recent research concluded, "few ex-patients who do not return to the hospital enjoy more than a marginally normal existence" (Martindale and Martindale, 1971:211). Many of the so-called cures depend on continuous drug intake.

A basic feature of the societal reaction to deviance is "blaming the victim" (Ryan, 1971). Whether the reaction is punitive or rehabilitative, a common belief is that unacceptable behavior is caused, entirely by the deviant. By looking only at the individual, social norms and institutions are ignored. Changing established practices can appear dangerous or difficult. Yet, the most severe or primary social problems may be within the basic structures of a society.

Stability and Change

According to the public opinion paradigm, social problems are conditions that many people consider undesirable. The definition implies that established, traditional beliefs and values are preferable to new, changed ones. Stability, order, and the status quo are the criteria of societal well-being from this perspective.

For primitive or undeveloped societies, stability has not only been a favored norm but also the actuality. For Western nations, during the past several centuries, social change has been more common (La Piere, 1965:1–2). Rapid growth of population, scientific discoveries, development of industry, expansion of commerce, democratization, and secularization are among the numerous changes. Since many of the innovations aroused substantial opposition, the public opinion paradigm suggests that they were social problems. Others may contend that some of the changes were improvements or solutions.

By *stability* is meant the continuation of accepted beliefs, values, practices, and social structures. Sociological theorists have tended to the belief that societies and individuals require stable relationships and institutions. This assumption is said to characterize functional analysis (Gouldner, 1970:251–254) and most sociological thinking (Lauer, 1973:3). Some sociologists see social change as a major cause of social problems.

Researchers have shown that some social problems are related to the stability or changes in society. Durkheim's 1899 study of suicide revealed that the lowest rates occurred during periods of economic stability (Durkheim, 1951:ch. V) and later studies tend to support his conclusions (Henry and Short, 1954:ch. 2; Maris, 1969:53–54).

Human beings and their societies require some kinds of stability. We need to know where our next meal is coming from and that our future is secure. We want reliable, faithful loved ones, friends, and leaders. Societies exist through stable languages, agreed-upon practices, and reliable institutions.

Stability is most preferable, obviously, for those who fear change. To the affluent, comfortable, or powerful, all change may seem to be for the worst. The unknown effects of change are frightening. The known effects can be losses in wealth, privilege, and influence.

Changes are sought when they offer benefits. Technological innovations are promoted for their economic rewards. They are favored by consumers when they seem useful or enjoyable. The advantages of antibiotics, electricity, and the automobile were fairly clear, but certain negative consequences—population growth, energy shortages, and traffic fatalities—were less evident.

Some changes are neither sought nor desired. Environmental disasters, including drought, floods, tornadoes, and earthquakes, produce many harmful effects. Also undesirable are such consequences of our social institutions and processes as economic recessions, military conflicts, and increases in traffic injuries. Few benefit from these changes.

An *innovation* is a change in ideas, customs, or social practices. The discovery of bacteria and the invention of the jet engine are examples. It has been said that necessity is the mother of invention. Certainly the perception of needs or problems encourages innovators. Still, needs vary. What is good for the public may not be so good for General Motors or the American Medical Association.

An illustration is the distribution of health care services. With the exception of the United States, modern countries have introduced some kind of national health service. Its advocates point to the low standing of the United States in international comparisons of tuberculosis deaths, infant mortality, and life expectancy. On such health indicators, the richest nation in the world is ranked between eighth and sixteenth. Needs do not result, inevitably, in innovations or solutions.

New ideas and techniques have been opposed or resisted. The first strikes in the United States were for a reduction of the workday to twelve hours. The preservation of slavery was a major issue in the Civil War. Public education, desegregation, women's right to vote, and social security for the aged were opposed by many people. Established customs and powerful institutions are especially resistant to the forces of change.

When old habits, ideas, and practices are overcome, new ones create new needs. In this sense, invention is the mother of necessity. The automobile, television, unemployment compensation, and public education have become necessities in the modern society.

Diffusion refers to changes that spread by contact and communication between peoples. Modern methods of transportation and media of communication have increased the diffusion of knowledge. The standards of advanced societies are known and desired by less advantaged peoples. Discontent over poverty, disease, and high death rates is a growing force for social change throughout the world. How to conserve the beneficial features of each society while achieving the gains of the others is a challenge to the world order.

Progress, Evolution, and Revolution

According to historian Charles A. Beard (1932:ix), "The world is largely ruled by ideas, true and false." Beard did not mean that beliefs, in themselves, can move mountains. He did mean that such beliefs may encourage people to strive to move mountains. The consequences may be despair or earth-moving machinery.

Our definitions of the situation play an important part in our behavior. If we think that our problems are unsolvable, it is not likely that we will act to solve them. If we think they can be solved, our efforts will be guided by our beliefs about them. We use what we think will work. The adequacy of our techniques and our resources determines the success or failure of our efforts.

An important modern belief is the *idea of progress.* In a classic book on this topic, a British historian, J. B. Bury (1932), asserted that the ancient world did not believe in the inevitability of progress. The Greeks and Romans thought that they lived in an era of decline and degeneration. During the Middle Ages, Christian belief in original sin was accompanied by faith in Divine Providence. Salvation was not to be found in this world but in heaven.

For Bury, the idea of progress assumed that the continuous improvement of humanity would result from advances in knowledge. During the eighteenth century, there were new equalitarian philosophies, great scientific discoveries, and substantial developments in commerce and industry. Prospects for the future appeared to be favorable and inevitable.

The idea of progress played an important part in theories of evolution and revolution. The term *evolution,* which I shall discuss first, is used in two different ways. Generally, it refers to gradual progress or improvement. To the scientific community, it means the specific theories derived from Spencer, Darwin, and their successors. I shall deal with the latter theories and their applications to social phenomena.

As we saw in Chapter 1, Darwin's theory stressed the struggle for survival and the process of natural selection. Individual characteristics favorable for survival were said to be carried on by the species through heredity. Unfavorable characteristics would die out, and, predictably the fittest would survive.

Social evolution was a central feature of the sociology of Herbert Spencer, a British contemporary of Darwin's. In 1862 Spencer wrote that societies evolved from homogeneous simplicity to heterogeneous complexity (1898). Among the products of social evolution were increased freedom and individuality. A necessary feature of evolution was competition between group members. To Spencer, helping the unfit would only delay the solution of social problems.

Although conflict was accepted as a feature of social evolution in the United States, many of the early sociologists believed in concerted action to solve problems (see House, 1936:ch. 26). Numerous books and articles were written in the 1920s and 1930s on evolutionary progress. Since then, the concepts of progress and evolution have almost disappeared from sociological discussions, although cultural anthropology continues to apply theories of social evolution (Duncan, 1964:49–61). Still, the idea of inevitable improvement seems implicit in such sociological conceptions as the natural history of social problems.

While historians and political scientists have devoted much attention to revolutionary change, few American sociologists have done so. Textbooks on social movements and collective behavior have focused upon groups seeking partial or gradual reform, such as women's rights or pensions for the aged. The topic of revolution is apt to be discussed in a few pages (see Turner and Killian, 1957:502–511; Lang and Lang, 1961:500–504).

To Marxists, gradual progress is punctuated by revolutions. Changes in the modes of production—as from agriculture to industry—result in societal improvement. In the *Communist Manifesto,* first published in 1847, Marx and Friedrich Engels pointed out the achievements of the bourgeoisie or business class. They asserted that the bourgeoisie had produced more useful innovations than all previous classes put together, among them, improved agriculture, machinery, railroads, and scientific discoveries.

Marx and Engels contended that progress has benefited, largely, the dominant class of each historic era. Exploitation of the proletariat, or working class, is central to the capitalist system. Just as the bourgeoisie had overthrown and replaced the aristocracy, the proletariat was expected to replace the bourgeoisie.

Since ruling classes do not voluntarily give up their

power and advantages, class struggle leads to violent methods. The revolutionary solution to exploitation and class conflict is communism—common ownership of the modes of production. All would be equal in a classless world.

Successful revolutions did not take place, as was predicted, in the advanced, industrial societies. Moreover, the communist nations have not eliminated inequalities of power and status. A new class of the higher political bureaucracy has emerged (Djilas, 1957:38). Freedom of speech and action has often been restricted.

Still, the industrial and economic benefits of communism are attractive to the many millions of poor, hungry, and powerless people of the world. In developed and underdeveloped nations, old and new theories and active advocates of revolution are widespread (Johnson, 1966: Woddis, 1972). International problems of food shortages, racial discrimination, and other forms of inequality can lead to revolutionary types of solutions.

I have suggested that poverty, racism, and war are among our serious social problems. In seeking to improve these conditions, we encounter the resistance of established practices and institutions. Obviously, better understanding of powerful social structures is needed. How to deal with them successfully and non-violently is a major challenge of our times.

The Active Society

Modern societies have large populations, elaborate technology, massive corporations, giant labor unions, and growing political bureaucracies. Effective functioning of complex societies and institutions requires careful planning and coordination. Producing a new line of automobile, such as the Ford Granada, was based upon years of preparation and the expenditure of many millions of dollars. Obtaining oil from Alaska followed conflict with environmentalists, government approval, moving thousands of workers, and billion-dollar investments. The effects of the decisions and actions on the participants and on the society, obviously, are substantial.

The power of gigantic organizations over the lives of their members as well as the rest of society is of increasing concern to all of us. Through propaganda, lobbying for legislation, and election of favored candidates, powerful organizations dominate societal decision-making. The secret, illegal political contributions revealed by the Watergate investigations are partial evidence of these influences.

The power of our federal, state, and local governments is great and growing. The federal bureaucracy employs nearly three million persons and the military forces almost three million more. Our federal budget costs us about $300 billion each year. (These data, and those that follow, are from the yearly *Statistical Abstract of the United States.*)

What do we get for our money? The largest amount, about $80 billion or more yearly, goes for military expenditures. Another $11 to $12 billion is spent each year for veterans of past wars. Interest on the federal debt accounts for more than $20 billion annually. About two-thirds of this debt resulted from World War II.

The second largest item in the federal budget is for what the government calls "income security." Nearly $70 billion each year are earmarked mainly for old-age and disability payments. These include returns to workers for their earlier contributions.

Billions of dollars are also spent on health, education, agriculture, commerce, space, and other federal programs. The desirability and efficiency of these programs are sources of public controversy. We know that they have not solved the problems of poverty, crime, segregation, and unemployment.

Policy decisions in governmental, business, and labor organizations are made by elected or appointed leaders. We are concerned with the question of who plans the planners. We are concerned also with the consequences of social policies for our social problems. These concerns are apparent in a proposed typology of societies.

In terms of social policy-making, Etzioni (1968:ch. 17) suggests that there are four types of societies. The *passive society* is one that does little to guide itself or involve its members. Knowledge is not used for planning, and the participation and consensus of members is limited. Underdeveloped nations are examples of passive societies.

Totalitarian countries are *overmanaged societies*, in which control and planning capacities may be used regularly. However, consensus-building or public acceptance is disregarded, and individual and group members are manipulated by those who hold power.

Capitalist democracies are more successful in achieving consensus than they are in controlling themselves. Public opinion is freer and open. However, policy-making offers limited guidance for its members. Such societies are *drifting societies*.

For Etzioni, the ideal society of the future will be the *active society*, a type that is effective both in planning and in consensus-building. Policies are designed not only to be effective but to encourage the active participation of its members. The term *self-guiding society* has been used to describe the active society (Breed, 1971).

Knowledge is an important element of the active society. Seeking and spreading knowledge is needed for societal guidance. Hence, Etzioni stresses the importance of research and education. When individual members do not agree with, or understand, group decisions and actions, they are resentful or alienated. When they are deceived or misled, they are even more frustrated and angered.

I believe that the idea of an active. self-guiding society

is a useful one. Solving social problems requires both knowledge and action. This combination has brought us many material advantages. Now we need to carefully study and take the needed actions to deal with our mounting social problems.

In these remarks, I do not claim that our task is easy or simple. Our knowledge about social behavior, institutions, and problems lags far behind our knowledge of physical and chemical phenomena. Group differences, complexity, and social change will continue to hamper our inquiries and our efforts. Differences in human interests, goals, and values will be substantial barriers to planning and consensus. Still, careful appraisal and application of the knowledge-values of science can help us to solve our serious social problems.

Toward Solutions

In terms of magnitude, poverty in the United States is a serious social problem. While definitions and criteria differ, twenty to thirty million Americans live below contemporary standards of diet, shelter, medical care, and similar conditions. About half of the poverty population are children or old people. They make up about two-thirds of our welfare population, since many adults are ineligible.

Poverty is here and now. By *solutions*, I mean activities that improve currently harmful conditions. Our present welfare system is costly, inefficient, and degrading. With it, many millions still live in poverty. A guaranteed annual wage and a negative income tax have been proposed as ways to reduce or eliminate the problem of poverty. A good question is whether we need to consider such major, costly solutions.

Instead of being concerned with such spurious or minor social problems as long hair, marihuana, or homosexuality, we should seek to solve more serious ones. Poverty is an appropriate example.

Poverty is not only substantial in magnitude but also in severity of consequences. Among its hypothesized or demonstrable effects are higher rates of mortality, ill-health, malnutrition, delinquency, dropouts, apathy, and dependency (see Will and Vatter, 1965; Seligman, 1968; Roach and Roach, 1974). These multiple consequences suggest that poverty is a primary social problem. We may predict that by reducing poverty, a reduction of other social problems will follow.

Attempts to solve problems can create new problems. During the 1920s, the prohibition of alcohol led to widespread lawbreaking, such as bootlegging and organized crime. Efforts to control pollution require costly devices and more automotive gasoline consumption. Affirmative-action laws increase work opportunities for women, blacks, and chicanos, but they reduce the opportunities for white males.

Determining the social costs and benefits of proposed solutions is a difficult matter. Perhaps even more difficult is implementing potential solutions. Those who benefit from poverty will resist changes that threaten to reduce their power, wealth, and privilege. The advantages include industry's reservoir of the unemployed, the farmer's migrant laborers, and the middle-class family's underpaid cleaning woman.

Improved knowledge is a requirement for successful problem-solving. For example, there are many erroneous ideas about poverty. A Boston study compared factual data with public beliefs about welfare. The author concluded that most people believed the welfare poor to be "more idle, more dishonest, and more fertile than they actually are" (Williamson, 1974:172).

There are many gaps in our knowledge of social problems. Interestingly, the federal government spends about ten times as much for defense and aerospace research as it does for all health, education, and welfare research (*Statistical Abstract of the United States*, 1973:524). While business and industry spend billions of dollars on product research, I hypothesize (for I have no data) that their research spending on poverty, crime, mental disorder, alcoholism, and other social problems is minute.

Our lack of knowledge about social problems is related, in part, to our values. As the preceding paragraph suggests, we usually pay only for what we want. There has been little real demand—in the economic sense of willingness to spend—for study or solutions of social problems. It is cheaper, and more common, for employers to dismiss emotionally troubled employees than to pay for their rehabilitation.

Appraising our values is another prerequisite of problem-solving. Some of our traditional values promote rather than reduce problems. An illustration is the value of punishment for undesirable behavior. Alcoholics or drug addicts are more apt to land in jail than receive rehabilitative assistance. The same is true for homosexuals. Criminalization is a possible outcome.

Racial prejudice is a source of many problems. Many northern whites were opposed to racial segregation—in the south. Since the black migration to northern cities, a massive exodus of whites to the suburbs has been taking place. One consequence is a new pattern of segregated northern schools and neighborhoods. Because more blacks than whites are poor, less educated, and unskilled, the central cities are losing the tax revenues needed to cope with urban slums and crime.

Knowledge, even of harmful consequences, does not readily change values or behavior. Most Americans are probably aware that smoking cigarettes is "dangerous to your health." While we assume that smokers value health and fear cancer, most continue their habit. Still, the required warning on each package and the legal ban on television advertising has been followed by a reversal of smoking trends. Cigarette sales were rising steadily until 1963. Since then, they declined—for a time. The American Cancer Society claims that more than twenty million persons have stopped smoking. About four out of five smokers said they hoped that their children would never smoke (Nuehring and Markle, 1974). Yet, tobacco usage and lung cancer remain widespread.

Achieving the value consensus needed for problem-solving need not imply intolerance of diversity. As evolutionists point out, social change promotes complexity and variety. An active society can encourage freedom and innovation. The limits of freedom, however, are the rights and well-being of others. That is, freedom depends on mutual responsibility. Encouraging others to adopt demonstrably harmful practices, as does tobacco advertising, is freedom for some and injury to others.

Social action based on improved knowledge and values is a final ingredient of problem-solving. An active society promotes useful, needed change. For our serious social problems, the appropriate changes involve our established practices, organizations, and institutions.

Our efforts to solve social problems encounter an old question. Which comes first—the chicken or the egg? Changing individuals or changing their conditions? In part, the argument is fallacious. At any given point in time, it can be one or the other. The answer depends upon the circumstances.

Some individuals are adaptable, others are not. The same is true for our institutions. Still, some sociologists contend that institutional changes are more likely to be successful. An example is the effort to reduce traffic injuries. Seat belts and speed laws are said to be more effective than driver education courses (Etzioni, 1972). Drug rehabilitation programs temporarily cure addicts. Slums readdict them.

We need not halt our efforts to help individuals. We also can try to alter social situations. Many of our social problems result from malfunctioning social structures. Solving the problems of poverty, crime, and addiction may require structural changes. Let us consider that possibility.

Structural Accountability

In the words of poet John Donne, "No man is an island." Throughout the world, human beings live with and depend on others. Our groups include our society, family, schools, businesses, and government. We call their organized patterns of relationships *social structure.* Among these patterns are goals, norms, rights, and obligations.

A characteristic of modern societies is their multiplicity of organizations and institutions. In the United States, there are many thousands of federal, state, and local governments and jurisdictions. They include administrative, law enforcement, educational, and public health organizations.

Our business world includes a variety of enterprises, private and corporative, local and multinational. Factory workers and professionals belong to labor unions or similar organizations. There are numerous associations: businessmen, military, physicians, and teachers. Less well organized—and less influential—are the poor, the aged, students, and the handicapped.

The importance of organizational efforts is recognized increasingly by disprivileged members of society. Since the 1960s, they have voiced appeals for student unity, women's liberation, black power, and chicano power. We have also seen anti-war, environmental, and consumer organizations.

Social structures are expected or assumed to satisfy human needs and wants. At times, however, they fail to do so. Instead of serving people, governments may waste taxes, restrict speech, or declare war. Families can be sources of unhappiness and mental disorders. Through planned obsolescence, manufacturers may dissatisfy buyers (see *Consumer Reports,* 1970 and 1971).

A study of governmental regulatory commissions and agencies reveals their shortcomings. According to the author, their "effect is almost always to enhance the position of the industry or licensed occupation at the expense of the public at large" (Pfeffer, 1974:478). The title of a recent book, *Making Institutions Work* (Vickers, 1973), suggests the concern of this section.

Vickers recognizes the importance, necessity, and utility of modern institutions. He points out that our great achievements in technology, agriculture, transportation, and communication depended upon the organized efforts of many people. Modern institutions provide such social benefits as widespread education, medical care, and social security.

To Vickers, a great task for all of us is understanding and controlling our institutional environment. He recommends that we examine public values and institutional policies. We need to know who gets what from these institutions—and why. Recognizing what our institutions do and can do is required for making them work.

Some institutions, like jails and mental hospitals, isolate deviants from society. *Total institutions* are places for individuals who have been brought together for punishment or treatment (Goffman, 1961). As we have already seen, they do not work well.

A total institution for drug addicts is the federal hospital at Lexington, Kentucky. Follow-up studies of its treated addicts show only brief success. Although no longer physically addicted upon release, from 75 to 95 percent of treated addicts returned to drugs within six months (Kittrie, 1973:239).

The high cost of obtaining narcotics leads addicts to other criminal behaviors. In the United States, the link between addiction and crime has led to stronger efforts at drug suppression and treatment. Informed observers contend that these attempts are self-defeating, pointing out that the drug-crime connection is virtually absent when drugs are controlled and available. This is the case in Great Britain and in some American methadone programs (Glaser, 1971).

So, what do we do? I have already noted, in Chapter 4, that we have begun to require accountability from our schools (see Barbee and Bouck, 1974). Taxpayers want their money's worth. Teachers want adequate salaries and facilities. Parents want their children to learn. Students want worthwhile, interesting instruction. Modern societies need informed, contributing, and responsible citizens.

Making schools work involves reconciling these different objectives. To do so, we have to understand and appraise such goals. We must find out more about what goes on in our schools. We should ask whether there are other and better ways to educate.

It is proper to ask similar questions about our other institutions. By *structural accountability* I mean careful public appraisal of the aims and procedures of societal structures. These include our political, military, educational, business, labor, and other organizations.

Among the important questions are: What can we expect our present institutions to do? How well do they serve our needs? What problems do they produce? What problems can they help us solve?

Toward Prevention

Which sounds better: An ounce of prevention is worth a pound of cure? Or, a gram of prevention is worth a kilogram of cure? Our system of weights and measures is outdated. Few modern nations retain it. Yet, the United States has moved very slowly toward the metric system. Established habits and institutions are hard to change.

Ideally, we ought to consider prevention before solutions of social problems. The critical problems of our time, however, cannot wait. We need to act now. Besides, the solution of social problems helps to prevent their continuation. Their solution also prevents other social problems. However, our current concerns must not mean neglect of tomorrow's potential problems.

I have said that solutions refer to existing problems. *Prevention* means avoiding problems before they occur. Still, the line between present and future is a moving one. As you read, the present slips into the past and is replaced by the future. That future concerns not only our own lifetimes but those of our children and grandchildren.

Looking and planning ahead does not imply the goals of some mythical Utopia. Dreams of perfect human beings in ideal societies are sources of inspiration. They should not distract us from impending realities. Daydreaming while getting ready to cross the street is a dangerous practice.

An illustration of the importance of prevention is the problem of war. Avoiding nuclear war is vitally necessary for all humanity. Such a war would be massively destructive. It is our most serious, potential problem.

Already there are five, and possibly more, nuclear powers. The capacity to produce nuclear weapons by other countries is on the increase. An added danger is that conflicts between non-nuclear nations could involve those that possess these weapons.

Each year the world community spends more on its military arsenals. The world's military spending exceeds $100 billion each year. About half or more is spent by the United States, one-fourth by Russia (Powell, 1973). The "war business" (Thayer, 1969) is big business. Hundreds of American communities depend on military contracts for profit, employment, and tax revenues.

For military advisers in each country, increased military expenditures seem necessary. To the critics, prevention of war means arms reduction. What seems desirable to individual nations endangers them all.

Another critical focus of prevention is that of rapid population increase. The world's population is now more than 3.8 billion. By the year 2000, it is expected to be about 6.5 or 7 billion. Unless this rapid population growth can be prevented, our future problems will reach tragic proportions. Current food shortages are likely to become famines in the poorer nations. Shortages of raw materials hold the threat of business failures and rising unemployment. More deaths, crimes, and riots are predictable outcomes.

In order to prevent these potential problems, we need to plan for the future. The success of our planning depends upon our ability for prediction. There are hazards in making such predictions.

Between 1900 and 1940, the birth rate in the United States was falling. Demographers expected the decline to continue. Some predicted that the American population would level off in 1950 at about 150 million people. Instead, birth rates increased, and our current population is more than 200 million—and rising. In the past few years, however, the birth rates have begun to fall once again.

Whatever the difficulties, societies and organizations try to plan ahead. Architects, engineers, and social scientists are initiating "images of the future" (Boulding, 1956; Polak, 1973). Their careful forecasts and reasoned alternatives are called *futurism* or *futurology*. Their publications now appear in reputable professional journals and in new ones such as *Futures* and *The Futurist*.

Sociologist Daniel Bell makes numerous forecasts in *The Coming of Post-Industrial Society* (1973). In general, he predicts wider application of knowledge for meeting human needs and dealing with social problems. Specifically, he foresees more jobs in service occupations than in industrial ones; less powerful corporations and more powerful government; greater use of professional and technical skills; and more education.

Reviewers do not disagree with his projections (see Bendix, 1974; Etzioni, 1974), pointing out that the predictions are based largely on already apparent trends. More serious is their view that Bell neglects the policy or value implications of social change. He seems to assume contemporary standards of judgment. In the words of a critic, Bell "has accepted the present world on its own terms" (Berger, 1974:105).

Preventing problems requires more than prediction. We need not wait blindly for the future to arrive. We can strive also to create the future (Huber, 1974). Prediction and planning are guides for social action.

Changing established structures can prevent the continuation of our present and our potential problems. Improving our prisons, mental institutions, families, and businesses would be helpful. We may also need to construct new institutions.

Institution building (Eaton, 1972) or *institution formation* means that "new institutions should be organized to help meet social needs where no institutions exist to solve the problems that people face and cannot resolve by themselves" (Etzkowitz, 1970:120). Much of our knowledge about institution building has come from American efforts to aid underdeveloped countries (Pooler and Duncan, 1972). Many new social structures have been initiated. They include agricultural enterprises, industries, and health care organizations.

Technically advanced societies have other needs and problems. Community Public Defenders or Ombudsmen could protect individuals against increasingly powerful organizations. A federal Peace Department might deter future pressures toward war. Subsidized child-care centers may prevent some of the growing problems of numerous working mothers. By developing such alternatives to our present structures, we can try to avoid or to limit our emerging problems.

Who Decides?

There is an old, anonymous saying that forty million Frenchmen can't be wrong, but a French sociologist Michael Crozier would probably disagree. He describes his country as a stalled society (1973), in which traditions and bureaucratic organizations tend to block solutions to important problems. Instead of promoting reforms, France seems to wait for revolutionary upheavals.

French leaders say that they advocate participation by the public. In reality, says Crozier, people are manipulated and misled. Many appear unconcerned. Crozier has no illusions about the "myth of participation." He sees no magic in mere numbers. Yet, he is also skeptical about the judgments of those who hold power over others. The dilemma is how to balance leadership and participation. To do so, he urges improved, widespread knowledge and joint action.

In this section, I shall use such views to conclude my discussion of social problems and their solutions. I have suggested that perceived social problems—what people consider undesirable—may be based on established values or those of influential elites. They may be based on knowledge or erroneous beliefs. They may lead to solutions or produce more harmful conditions.

On these grounds, I have proposed that sociologists attempt to distinguish spurious from demonstrable social problems, minor from serious ones. I have proposed that our criteria for these judgments be based on the knowledge-values of science. I have stressed also the provisional nature of scientific interpretations, of the possibility of scientific errors, and of the dangers of scientific domination.

I suggest that the knowledge-values of science offer appropriate criteria of social problems for sociologists. As social scientists, we should use such scientific criteria for distinguishing between subjective and objective knowledge. Knowledge of subjective beliefs is necessary for sociological analyses. Such beliefs need to be compared with more objective knowledge.

For many social problems, our knowledge is limited. We have much to learn about conflict, crime, family troubles, and racial prejudices. Our interpretations of these and other problem areas need to be cautious and hypothetical. Still, they are grounded on an accumulating body of facts and theories. They are preferable to unsupported or erroneous beliefs. They are more likely to produce successful solutions.

Whatever the state of our knowledge, we live and we act. Inaction is merely a passive form of action. Our behavior can be guided by impulse, emotion, tradition, or knowledge.

Our groups and societies are networks of active and passive members. Collectivities also may or may not be guided by knowledge. In the overmanaged, totalitarian nations, a self-selected few control knowledge and action. In drifting or stalled societies, knowledge is apt to be lacking or unused. A truly active society seeks and uses knowledge.

The most distinctive, and most controversial, aspect of my presentation concerns the place of values in defining social problems and in recommending solutions. Few will dispute the desirability of knowledge. More will question the scope and methods of scientific knowledge. Many more will doubt the possibility of a scientific basis for values.

Possible or not, scientists have started this search for new knowledge. Along with philosophers and theologians, they are questioning the split between facts and values. My statement of the knowledge-values of science is only one such effort. Like other scientific interpretations, it is a provisional one. It is open to appraisal, revision, or replacement.

My final question is, who decides? My answer is, you do. The basis of my answer is the conception of science as public knowledge. While the complexities of science are increasing, so too is public knowledge. Indeed, the growing influence of science on society requires wider public understanding of its contributions, its usages, and its limitations. Your study of social problems is part of your enlarging knowledge of science.

The knowledge-values of science need to be compared with knowledge from the arts and literature, religion and philosophy. They should be compared with the views of skilled practitioners—engineers, psychiatrists, urban planners, and other trained, experienced people. They should be compared, too, with the ideas and values of differing societies.

Proposing the widespread consideration of knowledge-values does not mean imposing them on others. To the contrary, they include freedom of inquiry and sharing of findings. Knowledge-values flourish in free societies. Determining their limits—our social responsibility—is part of the ongoing task of science and of society.

In his important book *Knowledge for What*, Robert S. Lynd cites the words of poet W. H. Auden. Lynd reminds sociologists about the dangers of "lecturing on navigation while the ship is going down" (1939:2). Our mounting social problems call for action guided by our best knowledge. It is time for our combined efforts to understand, prevent, and solve our serious social problems.

Summary

I have suggested that the knowledge-values of science offer criteria for studying, preventing, and solving social problems. However, we need to be aware of the limitations of scientific knowledge. These include the diversity of group values, the dangers of monopolized knowledge, the deficiencies in contemporary knowledge, and the changeability of social phenomena.

The term social control has been used to describe society's attempts to deter undesirable behavior. However, such supposed controls as imprisonment can have the harmful consequence of toughening inmates. Hence, some sociologists prefer the term societal reaction when describing the treatment of deviance.

From the public opinion perspective on social problems, stability seems to be the appropriate condition for societies. Social change is viewed, often, as a source of social troubles. Although progress or evolution was assumed by early sociologists, these conceptions are in less frequent use. Revolutionary change likewise receives scant attention.

Societies differ in their use of knowledge to solve problems and in participation by group members. On these grounds, there appear to be four types of societies—passive, overmanaged, drifting, and active ones. The active society promotes structural accountability toward prevention and solution of genuinely harmful conditions.

The knowledge-values of science can guide sociological efforts to identify and assess social problems. By applying and disseminating these knowledge-values, sociology can help to bridge the gap between an often uninformed public opinion and an effective public knowledge. Preventing and solving our serious social problems requires a participating and knowledgeable people.

RECOMMENDED READING

Bedau, Hugo, ed. *The Death Penalty in America.* Garden City, N.Y.: Anchor Books, 1964. A paperback anthology of provocative and informative studies.

Bell, Daniel. *The Coming of Post-Industrial Society.* New York: Basic Books, 1973. A comprehensive attempt to predict our emerging future.

Bierstedt, Robert. "Social Science and Public Policy." Pp. 412–20 in *Applied Sociology: Opportunities and Problems,* ed. Alvin W. Gouldner and S. M. Miller. New York: Free Press, 1965. In a few pages, the author presents a case for a value-free sociology in the service of public policy.

Breed, Warren. *The Self-Guiding Society.* New York: Free Press, 1971. This book is a shorter, slightly modified restatement of Etzioni's *The Active Society.* Easy to read and worthwhile.

Crozier, Michael. *The Stalled Society.* New York: Viking Press, 1973. While dealing with French problems, the book is applicable to other modern nations. The introduction, which deals with the responsibilities of the sociologist, raises important questions.

Etzioni, Amitai. *The Active Society.* New York: Free Press, 1968. A massive, informative, and difficult book, which proposes techniques for societal guidance.

Huber, Bettina J. "Some Thoughts on Creating the Future." *Sociological Inquiry,* 44 (1974):29–39. As the title suggests, the author urges that we plan actively for the future rather than merely predict and watch.

Jacoby, Neil H. "What Is a Social Problem?" *The Center Magazine* 4 (July-August 1971):35–40. Social problems are defined as gaps between public expectations and actual conditions. The author suggests that lowering these expectations can "solve" social problems.

Kittrie, Nicholas N. *The Right to Be Different: Deviance and Enforced Therapy.* Baltimore: Penguin Books, 1973. An expert on criminal law points out the dangers in our efforts to "rehabilitate" nonconformists.

Johnson, Chalmers. *Revolutionary Change.* Boston: Little, Brown, 1966. A study of the role of violence in social change.

Lauer, Robert H. *Perspectives on Social Change.* Boston: Allyn and Bacon, 1973. A useful introduction to this important topic.

Roach, Jack L., and Janet K. Roach, eds. *Poverty.* Baltimore: Penguin Books, 1972. A collection of articles on the causes, consequences, and proposed solutions to poverty.

Ryan, William. *Blaming the Victim.* New York: Pantheon Books, 1971. The author discusses the tendency to find fault with individuals rather than established social structures.

Toffler, Alvin, ed. *The Futurists.* New York: Random House, 1972. Social, biological, and physical scientists are among the well-known contributors to this paperback collection of articles.

Vickers, Geoffrey. *Making Institutions Work.* New York: Halsted Press, 1973. Although many examples refer to Great Britain, the book is applicable to other societies. A useful complement to the one by Ryan.

References

Acton, John Emerich. *Essays on Freedom and Power.* Boston: Beacon Press, 1949.

American Psychiatric Association. *Diagnostic and Statistical Manual: Mental Disorders.* Washington, D.C., 1968.

Barbee, David E., and Aubrey J. Bouck. *Accountability in Education.* New York: Petrocelli Books, 1974.

Barber, Bernard. *Science and the Social Order.* Glencoe, Ill.: Free Press, 1952.

Beard, Charles A. "Introduction" to J. B. Bury, *The Idea of Progress,* pp. ix–xl. New York: Macmillan, 1932.

Becker, Howard S. "Whose Side Are We On?" *Social Problems* 14 (Winter 1967): 239–47.

Bedau, Hugo, ed. *The Death Penalty in America.* Garden City, N.Y.: Anchor Books, 1964.

Bell, Daniel. *The Coming of Post-Industrial Society.* New York: Basic Books, 1973.

Bendix, Reinhard. "Review Symposium." *Current Sociology* 3 (March 1974): 99–101.

Beranek, William Jr., ed. *Science, Scientists, and Society.* Tarrytown-on-Hudson, N.Y.: Bogden and Quigley, 1972.

Berger, Stephen D. "Review Symposium." *Current Sociology* 3 (March, 1974): 101–5.

Bierstedt, Robert. "Social Science and Public Service." Pp. 412–20 in *Applied Sociology: Opportunities and Problems,* ed. Alvin W. Gouldner and S. M. Miller. New York: Free Press, 1965.

Blackmar, Frank W. *The Elements of Sociology.* New York: Macmillan, 1915.

Blume, Stuart S. *Toward a Political Sociology of Science.* New York: Free Press, 1974.

Blumer, Herbert. "Social Problems as Collective Behavior." *Social Problems* 18 (Winter 1971): 298–306.

———. "Society as Symbolic Interaction." Pp. in *Human Behavior and Social Processes,* ed. Arnold M. Rose. Boston: Houghton Mifflin, 1962.

———. *Symbolic Interactionism: Perspective and Method.* Englewood Cliffs, N.J.: Prentice-Hall, 1969.

Boulding, Kenneth. *The Image.* Ann Arbor: University of Michigan Press, 1956.

Brandt, Richard B. *Ethical Theory.* Englewood Cliffs, N.J.: Prentice-Hall, 1959.

Breed, Warren. *The Self-Guiding Society.* New York: Free Press, 1971.

Brown, Julia S., and Brian G. Gilmartin. "Sociology Today: Lacunae, Emphases, and Surfeits." *American Sociologist* 4 (November 1969): 283–91.

Brown, Martin, ed. *The Social Responsibility of the Scientist.* New York: Free Press, 1971.

Bruyn, Severyn T. *The Human Perspective in Sociology: The Methodology of Participant Observation.* Englewood Cliffs, N.J.: Prentice-Hall, 1966.

Bury, J. B. *The Idea of Progress.* New York: Macmillan, 1932.

Cattell, Raymond B. *A New Morality From Science: Beyondism.* New York: Pergamon Press, 1972.

Cicourel, Aaron V. *Method and Measurement in Sociology.* New York: The Free Press of Glencoe, 1964.

Clark, Ramsey. *Crime in America.* New York: Pocket Books, 1971.

Coleman, James S., et al. *Equality of Educational Opportunity.* Washington, D.C.: U.S. Government Printing Office, 1966.

Commoner, Barry. *The Closing Circle.* New York: Knopf, 1971.

Conant, James B. *Modern Science and Modern Man.* Garden City, N.Y.: Doubleday, 1953.

Consumers Union. *Consumer Reports.* Mount Vernon, N.Y.

Cooley, Charles H. *Social Organization.* New York: Scribner, 1909.

Cox, Edward F., Robert C. Fellmeth, and John C. Schulz. *The Nader Report on the Federal Trade Commission.* New York: Grove Press, 1969.

Crozier, Michael. *The Stalled Society.* New York: Viking Press, 1973.

Daniels, George H. *Science in American Society.* New York: Knopf, 1971.

de Lint, J. "Current Trends in the Prevalence of Excessive Alcohol Use and Alcohol-Related Health Damage" *The British Journal of Addiction* 70 (March 1975): 3–13.

Della Fave, L. Richard. "The Culture of Poverty Revisited: A Strategy for Research." *Social Problems* 21 (June 1974): 609–21.

Dentler, Robert A. *Basic Social Problems.* Chicago: Rand McNally, 1971.

Denzin, Norman K. *The Research Act.* Chicago: Aldine, 1970.

Deutscher, Irwin, *What We Say/What We Do.* Glenview, Ill.: Scott, Foresman, 1973.

Dewey, John. *Logic: The Theory of Inquiry.* New York: Henry Holt, 1938.

Dixon, Bernard. *What Is Science For?* London: William Collins, 1973.

Djilas, Milovan. *The New Class.* New York: Frederick A. Praeger, 1957.

Dohrenwend, Bruce P., and Barbara S. Dohrenwend. *Social Status and Psychological Disorder.* New York: Wiley, 1969.

Dressler, David, and Donald Carns. *Sociology: The Study of Human Interaction.* New York: Knopf, 1973.

Dubos, René. *Reason Awake: Science for Man.* New York: Columbia University Press, 1970.

Duncan, Otis Dudley. "Social Organization and the Ecosystem." Pp. 37–92 in *Handbook of Modern Sociology,* ed. Robert E. L. Faris. Chicago: Rand McNally, 1964.

Durkheim, Emile. *Suicide.* Glencoe, Ill.: Free Press, 1951.

Eaton, Joseph W. *Institution Building and Development.* Beverly Hills, Calif.: Sage Publications, 1972.

Eisenstadt, S. N., ed. *Comparative Social Problems.* New York: The Free Press of Glencoe, 1964.

Elliot, Henry C. "Similarities and Differences Between Science and Common Sense." Pp. 21–26 in *Ethnomethodology,* ed. Roy Turner. Baltimore: Penguin Books, 1974.

Ellis, Desmond, Harold G. Grasmick, and Bernard Gilman. "Violence in Prisons: A Sociological Analysis." *American Journal of Sociology* 80 (July 1974): 16–43.

Erikson, Kai T. "A Comment on Disguised Observation in Sociology." *Social Problems* 14 (Spring 1967): 366–73.

———. *Wayward Puritans.* New York: Wiley, 1966.

Etzioni, Amitai. "Review Symposium." *Current Sociology* 3 (March 1974): 105–7.

———."Human Beings Are Not Very Easy to Change After All." *Saturday Review,* Vol. 55, June 3, 1972, pp. 45–47.

———. *The Active Society.* New York: Free Press, 1968.

Etzkowitz, Henry. "Institution Formation Sociology." *American Sociologist* 5 (May 1970): 120–24.

Federal Bureau of Investigation. *Uniform Crime Reports.* Washington, D.C.: U.S. Government Printing Office, 1973.

Flacks, Richard. *Youth and Social Change.* Chicago: Rand McNally, 1971.

Flax, Michael J. *A Study in Comparative Urban Indicators: Conditions in Large Metropolitan Areas.* Washington, D.C.: The Urban Institute, 1972.

Frank, L. K. "Social Problems." *American Journal of Sociology* 30 (January 1925), 462–73.

Freeman, Howard E., and Wyatt C. Jones. *Social Problems: Causes and Controls.* Chicago: Rand McNally, 1973.

Friedrichs, Robert W. *A Sociology of Sociology.* New York: Free Press, 1970.

Fuller, Richard C. "The Problem of Teaching Social Problems." *American Journal of Sociology* 44 (November 1938): 415–25.

Fuller, Richard C. "Sociological Theory and Social Problems." *Social Forces* 15 (May 1937): 496–502.

———, and Richard R. Myers. "The Natural History of a Social Problem." *American Sociological Review* 6 (June 1941): 320–29.

Gallup, George H. *The Gallup Poll.* New York: Random House, 1972.

Gans, Herbert J. "The Positive Functions of Poverty." *American Journal of Sociology* 78 (September 1972): 275–89.

Garfinkel, Harold. "Conditions of Successful Degradation Ceremonies." *American Journal of Sociology* 61 (March 1956): 420–24.

———. *Studies in Ethnomethodology.* Englewood Cliffs, N.J.: Prentice-Hall, 1967.

Gerth, Hans, and C. Wright Mills. *Character and Social Structure.* New York: Harcourt, Brace and World, 1953.

Glaser, Daniel. "Criminology and Public Policy." *American Sociologist* 6 (June 1971): 30–37.

Gliner, Robert. *American Society as a Social Problem.* New York: Free Press, 1973.

Goffman, Erving. *Asylums.* Garden City, N.Y.: Anchor Books, 1961.

Goldsen, Rose K. "Mills and the Profession of Sociology." Pp. 88–93 in *The New Sociology,* ed. Irving L. Horowitz. New York: Oxford University Press, 1965.

Goode, Erich, ed. *Marijuana.* New York: Atherton Press, 1969.

Gouldner, Alvin W. *The Coming Crisis of Western Sociology.* New York: Basic Books, 1970.

———, and S. M. Miller, eds. *Applied Sociology: Opportunities and Problems.* New York: Free Press, 1965.

Gove, Walter R. "Societal Reaction as an Explanation of Mental Illness: An Evaluation." *American Sociological Review* 35 (October 1970): 873–84.

Green, Bert F. "Attitude Measurement." Pp. 335–69 in *Handbook of Social Psychology,* Vol. I, ed. Gardner Lindzey. Reading, Mass.: Addison-Wesley, 1954.

Greenberg, Daniel S. *The Politics of Pure Science.* New York: New American Library, 1967.

Gross, Llewellyn. "Values and Theory of Social Problems." Pp. 383–97 in *Applied Sociology,* ed. Alvin W. Gouldner and S. M. Miller. New York: Free Press, 1965.

Grupp, Stanley E., ed. *Marihuana.* Columbus, Ohio: Charles E. Merrill, 1971.

Guttenberg, Marcia. "The Relationship of Unemployment to Crime and Delinquency." *Journal of Social Issues* 26 (1968): 105–14.

Guttman, Louis. "Social Problems Indicators." *Annals of the American Academy of Political Science* 393 (January 1971): 40–46.

Haberer, Joseph. *Politics and the Community of Science.* New York: Van Nostrand Reinhold, 1969.

Hagstrom, Warren. *The Scientific Community.* New York: Basic Books, 1965.

Hartman, Robert S. *The Structure of Value.* Carbondale, Ill.: Southern Illinois University Press, 1967.

Heilbroner, Robert L. *The Worldly Philosophers.* New York: Simon and Schuster, 1953.

Henry, Andrew F., and James F. Short, Jr. *Suicide and Homicide.* New York: Free Press of Glencoe, 1954.

Henslin, James M., and Larry T. Reynolds, eds. *Social Problems in American Society.* Boston: Holbrook Press, 1973.

Hewitt, John P., and Peter M. Hall. "Social Problems, Problematic Situations, and Quasi-Theories." *American Sociological Review* 38 (June 1973): 367–74.

Horton, Paul B., and Gerald R. Leslie. *The Sociology of Social Problems.* Englewood Cliffs, N.J.: Prentice-Hall, 1974.

House, Floyd N. *The Development of Sociology.* New York: McGraw-Hill, 1936.

Huber, Bettina J. "Some Thoughts on Creating the Future." *Sociological Inquiry* 44 (1974): 29–39.

Irwin, John. "Participant-Observation of Criminals." Pp. 117–36 in *Research on Deviance,* ed. Jack D. Douglas. New York: Random House, 1972.

Jacoby, Neil H. "What Is a Social Problem?" *The Center Magazine* 4 (July–August, 1971): 35–40.

Jaeger, Gertrude, and Philip Selznick. "A Normative Theory of Culture." *American Sociological Review* 29 (October 1964): 653–68.

Jaffee, Jerome. "The Medical View" in *Marijuana,* ed. Erich Goode. New York: Atherton Press, 1969.

Jiobu, Robert M., and Carol A. Pollis. "Student Evaluations of Courses and Instructors." *American Sociologist* 6 (November 1971): 317–21.

Johnson, Chalmers. *Revolutionary Change.* Boston: Little, Brown, 1966.

Kaplan, Norman. "Sociology of Science." Pp. 852–81 in *Handbook of Modern Sociology,* ed. Robert E. L. Faris. Chicago: Rand McNally, 1964.

Kavolis, Vyautas, ed. *Comparative Perspectives on Social Problems.* Boston: Little, Brown, 1969.

Killian, Lewis M. *The Impossible Revolution.* New York: Random House, 1968.

Kinch, John W., ed. *Social Problems in the World Today.* Reading, Mass.: Addison-Wesley, 1974.

Kittrie, Nicholas. *The Right to Be Different*. Baltimore: Penguin Books, 1973.

Krohn, Roger G. *The Social Shaping of Science*. Westport, Conn: Greenwood, 1971.

Kuhn, Thomas S. *The Structure of Scientific Revolutions*. Chicago. University of Chicago Press, 1970.

Lang, Kurt, and Gladys E. Lang. *Collective Dynamics*. New York: Thomas Y. Crowell, 1961.

La Piere, Richard T. *Social Change*. New York: McGraw-Hill, 1965.

Lapp, Ralph E. *The New Priesthood: The Scientific Elite and the Uses of Power*. New York: Harper, 1965.

Lauer, Robert H. *Perspectives on Social Change*. Boston: Allyn and Bacon, 1973.

Lemert, Edwin M. "Social Problems." *The International Encyclopedia of Social Science* 14 (1968): 452–59.

———. *Social Pathology*. New York: McGraw-Hill, 1951.

Liebow, Elliot. *Tally's Corner*. Boston: Little, Brown, 1967.

Lingeman, Richard R. *Drugs from A to Z: A Dictionary*. New York: McGraw-Hill, 1969.

Liska, Allen E. "Emergent Issues in the Attitude-Behavior Controversy." *American Sociological Review* 39 (April 1974): 261–72.

Lowry, Ritchie P. *Social Problems*. Lexington, Mass.: Heath, 1974.

Lynd, Robert S. *Knowledge for What*. Princeton N.J.: Princeton University Press, 1948.

Manis, Jerome G. "Assessing the Seriousness of Social Problems." *Social Problems* 22 (October 1974): 1–15.

———. "The Concept of Social Problems: Vox Populi and Sociological Analysis." *Social Problems* 21 (1974): 305–15.

Mann, Kenneth W. *Deadline for Survival: A Survey of Moral Issues in Science of Medicine*. New York: Seabury Press, 1970.

Mannheim, Karl. *Ideology and Utopia*. New York: Harcourt, Brace, 1936.

Maris, Ronald W. *Social Forces in Urban Suicide*. Homewood, Ill.: Dorsey Press, 1969.

Marsh, Robert M. *Comparative Sociology*. New York: Harcourt, Brace and World, 1967.

Martindale, Don, and Edith Martindale. *The Social Dimensions of Mental Illness, Alcoholism, and Drug Dependence*. Westport, Conn.: Greenwood, 1971.

Marx, Karl, and Friedrich Engels. *The German Ideology*. New York: International Publishing, 1947.

Mauss, Armand. *Social Problems as Social Movements*. Philadelphia: Lippincott, 1975.

Mead, George H. *Mind, Self and Society*. Chicago: University of Chicago Press, 1934.

————. *On Social Psychology,* ed. Anselm Strauss, Chicago: University of Chicago Press, 1956.

Means, Richard L. *The Ethical Imperative: The Crisis in American Values.* Garden City N.Y.: Doubleday, 1969.

Meltzer, Bernard N. "Mead's Social Psychology." Pp. 4–22 in *Symbolic Interaction,* ed. Jerome G. Manis and Bernard N. Meltzer. Boston: Allyn and Bacon, 1972.

Merton, Robert K. *The Sociology of Science: Theoretical and Empirical Investigations.* Chicago: University of Chicago Press, 1973.

————. "Social Problems and Sociological Theory." Pp. 793–845 in *Contemporary Social Problems,* ed. Robert K. Merton and Robert Nisbet. New York: Harcourt Brace Jovanovich, 1971.

————. *Science, Technology and Society in Seventeenth Century England.* New York: Howard Fertig, 1970.

————. *Social Theory and Social Structure.* Glencoe, Ill.: Free Press, 1949. (Revised, 1957).

————. "Social Structure and Anomie." *American Sociological Review* 3 (October 1938): 672–82.

Michaelis, Anthony R., and Hugh Harvey, eds. *Scientists in Search of Their Conscience.* New York: Springer-Verlag, 1973.

Mill, J. Stuart. *A System of Logic.* New York: Longmans, Green, 1947.

Miller, Libuse L. *Knowing, Doing, and Surviving.* New York: Wiley, 1973.

Mills, C. Wright. *The Sociological Imagination.* New York: Grove Press, 1961.

————. *The Causes of World War Three.* New York: Ballantine Books, 1958.

————. *The Power Elite.* New York: Oxford University Press, 1957.

————. "The Professional Ideology of Social Pathologists." *American Journal of Sociology* 49 (September 1943): 165–80.

Mirande, Alfred M. *The Age of Crisis.* New York: Harper and Row, 1975.

Mitroff, Ian. "Norms and Counter-Norms in a Select Group of the Apollo Moon Scientists: A Case Study of the Ambivalence of Scientists." *American Sociological Review* 39 (August 1974): 579–95.

Monod, Jacques. "On the Logical Relationship Between Knowledge and Values." Pp. 11–23 in *The Biological Revolution: Social Good or Social Evil,* ed. Watson Fuller. Garden City, N.Y.: Doubleday, 1972.

Morris, Charles W. *Varieties of Human Value.* Chicago: University of Chicago Press, 1952.

Mueller, John H., Karl F. Schuessler, and Herbert L. Costner. *Statistical Reasoning in Sociology.* Boston: Houghton Mifflin, 1970.

Nagel, Ernest. *The Structure of Science*. New York: Harcourt, Brace and World, 1961.

Nagel, Stuart S. "The Tipped Scales of American Justice." Pp. 241–44 in *Critical Issues in the Study of Crime*, ed. Simon Dinitz and Walter C. Reckless. Boston: Little, Brown, 1968.

National Center for Health Statistics. *Reporting of Hospitalization in the Health Interview Survey*. Series 2, No. 6. Washington D.C.: U.S. Government Printing Office, 1965.

National Science Foundation. *American Science Manpower, 1970*. Washington, D.C.: U.S. Government Printing Office, 1971.

Nisbet, Robert A. *The Sociological Tradition*. New York: Basic Books, 1966.

———. "The Study of Social Problems." Pp. 1–25 in *Contemporary Social Problems*, ed. Robert K. Merton and Robert Nisbet. New York: Harcourt Brace Jovanovich, 1971.

Nuehring, Elaine, and Gerald E. Markle. "Nicotine and Norms: The Re-Emergence of a Deviant Behavior." *Social Problems* 21 (April 1974): 513–26.

Ogburn, William F. *Social Change*. New York: B. W. Huebsch, 1922.

Paddock, William and Paul. *Famine—1975!* Boston: Little, Brown, 1967.

Parsons, Talcott. *The Social System*. Glencoe, Ill.: Free Press, 1951.

———. *The Structure of Social Action*. New York: McGraw-Hill, 1937.

Pepper, Stephen C. "Survival Value." Pp. 107–14 in *Human Values and Natural Science*, ed. Ervin Laszlo and James B. Wilbur. New York. Gordon and Breach Science Publishers, 1970.

———. *A Digest of Purposive Values*. Berkeley: University of California Press, 1947.

Perrucci, Robert, and Marc Pilisuk. *The Triple Revolution Emerging*. Boston: Little, Brown, 1971.

Pfeffer, Jeffrey. "Administrative Regulation: Social Problem or Solution?" *Social Problems* 21 (April 1974): 468–79.

Phillips, Bernard S. *Social Research*. New York: Macmillan, 1971.

Polak, Fred. *The Image of the Future*. San Francisco: Jossey-Bass, 1973.

Pooler, William S., and Richard L. Duncan. "Technical Assistance and Institution Building: An Empirical Test." Pp. 183–225 in *Institution Building and Development*, ed. Joseph W. Eaton. Beverly Hills, Calif.: Sage Publications, 1972.

Powell, Elwin H. "Paradoxes of the Warfare State." Pp. 15–27 in *Peace and the War Industry*, ed. Kenneth E. Boulding. New Brunswick, N.J.: Transaction Books, 1973.

Queen, Stuart A., and Jennette R. Gruener. *Social Pathology: Obstacles to Social Participation*. New York: Thomas Y. Crowell, 1945.

————., and Delbert M. Mann. *Social Pathology.* New York: Thomas Y. Crowell, 1925.

Reissman, Leonard. "The Solution Cycle of Social Problems." *American Sociologist* 7 (February 1972): 7–9.

Reynolds, Larry T., and Janice M. Reynolds. *The Sociology of Sociology.* New York: McKay, 1970.

Reynolds, Paul D. *A Primer in Theory Construction.* Indianapolis: Bobbs-Merrill, 1971.

Richter, Maurice N. *Science as a Cultural Process.* Cambridge, Mass: Schenkman, 1972.

Roach, Jack L., and Janet K. Roach, eds. *Poverty.* Baltimore: Penguin Books, 1972.

Roberts, Walter O. "Science, A Wellspring of Our Discontent." *Science* 55 (March 1967): 3–14.

Rose, Arnold. *The Power Structure.* New York: Oxford University Press, 1967.

Ross, Edward A. *Social Control.* New York: Macmillan, 1901.

Rossi, Peter H., Emily Waite, Christine Bose, and Richard E. Berk. "The Seriousness of Crimes: Normative Structure and Individual Differences." *American Sociological Review* 39 (April 1974): 224–337.

————, and Walter Williams, eds. *Evaluating Social Programs.* New York: Seminar Press, 1972.

Rothman, David J. *The Discovery of the Asylum.* Boston: Little Brown, 1971.

Rubington, Earl, and Martin S. Weinberg. *The Study of Social Problems.* New York: Oxford University Press, 1971.

Ryan, William. *Blaming the Victim.* New York: Pantheon, 1971.

Salomon, Jean Jacques. *Science and Politics.* London: Macmillan, 1973.

Scheff, Thomas. *Being Mentally Ill.* Chicago: Aldine, 1966.

————. "The Societal Reaction to Deviance: Ascriptive Elements in the Psychiatric Screening of Mental Patients in a Midwestern State." *Social Problems* 11 (Spring 1964): 401–13.

Schur, Edwin M. *Labeling Deviant Behavior.* New York: Harper & Row, 1971.

————. *Crimes Without Victims.* Englewood Cliffs, N.J.: Prentice-Hall, 1965.

Seligman, Ben B., ed. *Aspects of Poverty.* New York: Thomas Y. Crowell, 1968.

Sellin, Thorsten, and Marvin E. Wolfgang. *The Measurement of Delinquency.* New York: Wiley, 1964.

Sewell, William H., and J. Michael Armer. "Neighborhood Context and College Plans." *American Sociological Review* 31 (April 1966): 159–68.

Sibley, Elbridge. *The Education of Sociologists in the United States.* New York: Russell Sage Foundation, 1963.

Simmons, J. L. *Deviants.* Glendessary Press, 1969.

Skinner, B. F. *Beyond Freedom and Dignity.* New York: Bantam Books, 1952.

Skolnick, Jerome H. *Justice without Trial.* New York: Wiley, 1967.

——, and Elliott Currie. *Crisis in American Institutions.* Boston: Little, Brown, 1973.

Smith, Cecil Blanche Woodham. *The Reason Why.* New York: McGraw-Hill, 1953.

Spencer, Herbert. *First Principles.* New York: Appleton, 1898.

Steffens, Lincoln. *The Autobiography of Lincoln Steffens.* New York: Harcourt, Brace, 1931.

Stewart, Elbert W. *The Troubled Land.* New York: McGraw-Hill, 1972.

Stinchcombe, Arthur L. *Constructing Social Theories.* New York: Harcourt, Brace and World, 1968.

Strauss, Leo. "Natural Right and the Distinction Between Facts and Values." Pp. 419–57 in *Philosophy of the Social Sciences: A Reader,* ed. Maurice Natanson. New York: Random House, 1963.

Sullivan, J. W. N. *The Limitations of Science.* New York: New American Library, 1949.

Sumner, William Graham. *Folkways.* Boston: Ginn, 1906.

Sutherland, Edwin H., and Donald R. Cressey. *Criminology.* Philadelphia: Lippincott, 1970.

Sykes, Gresham. *Social Problems in America.* Glenview, Ill.: Scott, Foresman, 1971.

Szasz, Thomas S. *The Myth of Mental Illness.* New York: Paul B. Hoeber, 1961.

Szymanski, Albert. "Military Spending and Economic Stagnation." *American Journal of Sociology* 79 (July 1973): 1–14.

Tallman, Irving, and Reese McGee. "Definition of a Social Problem." Pp. 19–58 in *Handbook on the Study of Social Problems,* ed. Erwin O. Smigel. Chicago: Rand McNally, 1971.

Taylor, Ian, Paul Walton, and Jock Young. *The New Criminology: For A New Theory of Deviance.* London: Routledge and Kegan Paul, 1973.

Thayer, George. *The War Business.* New York: Simon and Schuster, 1969.

Theodorson, George A., and Achilles G. Theodorson. *A Modern Dictionary of Sociology.* New York: Thomas Y. Crowell, 1969.

Thomas, William I. *The Child in America.* New York: Knopf, 1928.

————, and Florian Znaniecki. *The Polish Peasant in Europe and America.* New York: Knopf, 5 vols., 1918–1921; revised, 2 vols., 1927.

Tittle, Charles R. "Prisons and Rehabilitation: The Inevitability of Disfavor." *Social Problems* 21 (1974): 385–95.

Turner, Jonathan H. *The Structure of Sociological Theory.* Homewood, Ill.: Dorsey Press, 1974.

Turner, Ralph H., and Lewis M. Killian. *Collective Behavior.* Engelwood Cliffs: N.J.: Prentice-Hall, 1957.

Turner, Roy, ed. *Ethnomethodology.* Baltimore: Penguin Books, 1974.

United States Department of Health, Education and Welfare. *Toward a Social Report.* Ann Arbor, Mich.: University of Michigan Press, 1970.

Vickers, Geoffrey. *Making Institutions Work.* New York: Wiley, 1973.

Walter, Edward F. "The Rationality of Facts and Values." Pp. 119–31 in *Human Values and Natural Science,* ed. Ervin Laszlo and James B. Wilbur. New York: Gordon and Breach Science Publishers, 1970.

Webb, Eugene J., Donald T. Campbell, Richard D. Schwartz, and Lee Sechrest. *Unobtrusive Measures: Non-Reactive Research in the Social Sciences.* Chicago: Rand McNally, 1966.

Weber, Max. *The Protestant Ethic and the Spirit of Capitalism,* tr. Talcott Parsons. New York: Scribner, 1958.

————. *The Methodology of the Social Sciences,* tr. Edward A. Shils and Henry A. Finch. Glencoe, Ill.: Free Press, 1949.

White, Leslie A. *The Science of Culture.* New York: Grove Press, 1949.

Whitehead, A. N. *Science and the Modern World.* New York: Pelican Mentor Books, 1948.

Will, Robert E., and Harold G. Vetter, eds. *Poverty in Affluence.* New York: Harcourt, Brace and World, 1965.

Williamson, John B. "Beliefs About the Welfare Poor." *Sociology and Social Research* 58 (January 1974): 163–75.

Woddis, Jack. *New Theories of Revolution.* New York: International Publishers, 1972.

Ziman, J. M. *Public Knowledge.* Cambridge, Eng.: Cambridge University Press, 1968.

Index